D1554452

We Built Reality

We Built Reality

How Social Science Infiltrated

Culture, Politics, and Power

JASON BLAKELY

OXFORD
UNIVERSITY PRESS

OXFORD
UNIVERSITY PRESS

Oxford University Press is a department of the University of Oxford. It furthers
the University's objective of excellence in research, scholarship, and education
by publishing worldwide. Oxford is a registered trade mark of Oxford University
Press in the UK and certain other countries.

Published in the United States of America by Oxford University Press
198 Madison Avenue, New York, NY 10016, United States of America.

Library of Congress Cataloging-in-Publication Data
Names: Blakely, Jason, 1980- author.
Title: We built reality : how social science infiltrated culture, politics,
and power / Jason Blakely.
Description: New York, NY : Oxford University Press, [2020] |
Includes bibliographical references and index.
Identifiers: LCCN 2019053611 (print) | LCCN 019053612 (ebook) |
ISBN 9780190087371 (hardback) | ISBN 9780190087388 (paperback) |
ISBN 9780190087401 (epub) | 9780190087395 (updf) | 9780190087418 (online)
Subjects: LCSH: Social sciences—Study and teaching—United States. |
Scientism. | Pseudoscience—Social aspects—United States.
Classification: LCC H62.5. U5 .B53 2020 (print) | LCC H62. 5.U5 (ebook) |
DDC 300.973—dc23
LC record available at https://lccn.loc.gov/2019053611
LC ebook record available at https://lccn.loc.gov/2019053612

To Lindsay and to Sebastian—I carry you in my heart.

Frightful must it be; for supremely frightful would be the effect of any human endeavor to mock the stupendous mechanism of the Creator of the world.

—MARY SHELLEY, author's introduction, *Frankenstein* (1831)

CONTENTS

ACKNOWLEDGMENTS

The creation of this book owes an enormous intellectual debt to another political theorist and my former teacher, Mark Bevir. This is not to say he would agree with my positions here. But he helped me to grasp the importance of interpretation in the social sciences when I was his student at the University of California, Berkeley. Later we defended this approach together in a book entitled *Interpretive Social Science*.

I also wish to thank the various teachers and friends I have had over the years who opened up the humanities, history, and literature as a profound way of understanding the world, including David Albertson, Mitch Miller, Andrew Davison, Andrew K. Bush, Giovanna Borradori, Rachel Kitzinger, Charles Dunn, my parents, and numerous others. My colleagues and students at Pepperdine University—even if not always in agreement with me—often expanded my sense of both the social sciences and the humanities; John Barton, Paul Contino, Bryant Crubaugh, Dan Morrison, Chris Soper, and Robert Williams deserve special mention. The men and women at Daniel's Place in Santa

Monica deepened my engagement with poetry and were essential to my encounter with the poems quoted in these pages. T. J. Berden and Matthew Miller pushed me to speak to the politics of the hour. More concretely, I am grateful to Péter Róna and Blackfriars Hall, Oxford, for the invitation to speak at a symposium that helped me develop some of the ideas that fed into chapters 1 and 2; Chase Mendoza for collaboration on research that contributed to the insights of chapter 2; Tim Rappold and James Abraham for critically reading an early draft of chapter 3; and Lindsay Blakely for her extremely thoughtful and intelligent editing throughout. AMDG.

INTRODUCTION: ELECTION DAY 2016

On November 8, 2016, Americans were on edge. A campaign season of unusual vitriol and unprecedented departures from civic decency and constitutional norms was culminating in a tight race. Yet among the small group of statistics wonks whose job it was to scientifically predict election results, the mood was self-assured. The most popular forecasters agreed that the former senator from New York, Hillary Rodham Clinton, would become the next president of the United States. Newspapers and television broadcasts across the country repeated the claim. Nate Cohn of the *New York Times*; Nate Silver of *FiveThirtyEight.com*; and scientific forecasters from the *Huffington Post, PredictWise*, and other authoritative outlets had all reached the same conclusion.

On the morning of November 8, Cohn, one of the country's most esteemed forecasters, announced an 85 percent chance that Clinton would win (her chances of losing were "about the same probability that an N.F.L. kicker misses a 37-yard field goal," his website helpfully explained). The Princeton Election Consortium (PEC) went even further, placing Clinton's probability of winning between 98 and 99 percent. In other words, Donald Trump's odds of becoming the next president of the United States were literally approaching one in a hundred. Such calculations led Samuel Wang—the director of the PEC and a Stanford University–trained neuroscientist—to publicly announce in October that the presidential contest was already "totally over." "If Trump wins more than 240 electoral votes," he wrote, "I will eat a bug."

In the years leading up to the 2016 election, Americans had lavished large sums of money and attention on self-proclaimed social scientific forecasters like Wang, Silver, and Cohn. These prediction gurus used methods and data developed by academics (including statistical regressions and demographic aggregations) to foretell political and economic futures. Such prediction gurus built personal brands, ran massive websites, and sold books based on their ability to statistically detect "signals" of future outcomes amid the wider informational "noise" of society. Yet as the first results of the vote came in on Election Day 2016, these forecasters changed their percentages with dizzying speed. Cohn's website, for example, flipped from predicting in the afternoon an 85 percent chance of Clinton winning to predicting by nightfall a 95 percent chance of Trump winning.

Average citizens, doing their best to remain informed, were completely dumbfounded. They may not have understood the technicalities of statistical science, but surely some chicanery was afoot. In an election largely cast as a referendum on societal elites, yet another form of elite expert authority appeared to have failed spectacularly. Indeed, so total was the consensus among elite opinion that some have even speculated that the Trump campaign had shown signs of not believing he would win.[1] How could these election forecasters—celebrated gurus in the science of voter behavior—be so wrong? How could the chance of Clinton winning change in a matter of hours from that of an NFL kicker missing a routine field goal to less than drawing an ace from a deck of shuffled cards?

In the following weeks the astounding blunders of the nation's most popular election experts led to a public debate. Was the problem the methods of the forecasters, or was it the entire enterprise of forecasting human behavior more generally? Those whose business it was to scientifically track and predict elections sought explanations that might salvage their authority. Many came to the conclusion that the fault was not theirs; social scientific authority had been distorted and abused by the popular media. Others, like the Pew Research Center, argued that the accuracy of the polling had been foiled by the surprise phenomenon of "shy Trumpers" or voters too embarrassed about their support for Trump to give an accurate account to pollsters. This had created faulty survey data that were then fed into the statistical models and calculations, botching the predictions.

What few considered was that the failure of election forecasting might not be an isolated incident but instead symptomatic of a wider cultural problem: scientism or granting undue authority to scientific methods. And yet social scientists had spent much of the preceding decades failing to predict everything from massive economic recessions to the collapse of entire empires (episodes I revisit in these pages). While social scientific authority had largely failed to predict the nature of the world at the beginning of the twenty-first century, it had nevertheless played a key role in creating it. Many of the theories that were unable to predict crisis after crisis were the very theories that helped construct crisis after crisis. Or at least this is one of the suggestions of this book: that social science can undergo a strange metamorphosis in our societies and become its opposite, ideology and superstition.

Most social science researchers never reflect on the role of scientism in their own work, let alone the way that their paradigms, theories, and models are taken over by popular forms of belief, practice, culture, and power. Indeed, seeing the world in this way requires a certain heterodox way of looking at social scientific texts—not as dry, technical tracts describing the world but as vividly cultural and ideological meanings that endeavor to transform the world. This is the (almost) lost art of interpreting the meanings of social science and considering the different ways in which they are embodied in the world. As a form of understanding more familiar to scholars in the humanities, this interpretive way of reading is often dismissed as irrelevant by social scientists in their rush to consider more "concrete" empirical matters. This is one reason the problem of scientism is rarely if ever perceived, let alone discussed, by social scientists themselves. Vulgar misreadings of their tracts are just that.

A major doctrine that has blocked this way of reading social science texts is the widespread view that social scientists are conducting a form of research akin to that in the natural sciences. Most social scientists either ignore or deny the ideological and moral implications of their own theories. Indeed, they even hold that their theories are logically distinct from evaluative and prescriptive claims, instead engaging strictly in forms of factual assertion and description. Over the course of this book I argue that this long-standing distinction between description and prescription, fact and value, is far more complex and porous than this venerable dogma (traceable to the great empirical philosopher David Hume) would have one believe.

Indeed, the pages of this book show that social science has played an important role in creating new ethical, political, and ideological meanings. Contemporary social science is a veritable factory of meanings, every bit as dynamic, poetical, and fecund as a creative writing department. Contemporary social science has also helped spread the scientism that now dominates many of our most powerful institutions and even the minutiae of our personal lives. These themes shape the central thesis of this book: that social science rarely simply neutrally describes the world, but rather plays a role in constructing and shaping it. In other words, the social sciences are not like the classic natural sciences (physics, chemistry, biology, etc.), in which descriptions of the world do not directly alter and reshape it. Because humans inhabit worlds of meaning, and social scientific theories are in part expressions of novel meanings, those theories can always penetrate human understanding and radically alter the very societies they seek to describe. But to see this we need to make a radical paradigm shift in how we read the genre of social science, not simply as an empirical exercise but as a form of cultural and ideological production.

This book introduces readers to the art of reading social science in this neglected way—what philosophers call a hermeneutic or interpretive approach, which I explain shortly. This book also offers a roadmap of how social science helped build the world we currently inhabit, a world of scientism in everything from our practices of courtship to the way we police our neighborhoods.

Scientism forms nothing less than a uniquely modern type of culture and power. Where earlier societies suffered abuses of various kinds of authority—clerical, political, tribal, and familial—modern societies alone experience the abuse of authority in the name of science.

The first two chapters examine how a vision of human beings popularized by economics has helped to radically restructure our society into what I call a "market polis." The market polis is largely responsible for the self-defeating responses by politicians, policy makers, pundits, and ordinary citizens to the 2008 recession and the runaway inequality that threatens to topple today's democracies. This popular economic way of thinking has entered nearly every domain of life through metaphors of society as a self-correcting, equilibrium machine and humans as rational calculators. Chapters 3 and 4 shift focus to the culture of scientism's effects on our self-conceptions and our increasing treatment of ourselves and others as manipulable machines. The social scientific theories fueling this shift in popular practice emerge out of cognitive psychology, behavioral genetics, and various other social sciences that help construct an extended metaphor of humans as machines or *homo machina*. Finally, chapters 5 and 6 examine how both domestically and internationally, the United States has developed social scientific theories that supposedly uniquely justify the exercise of violence. Here social science has been popularly recruited through the "law and order" movement to build a new, subtle form of racial hierarchy at home while constructing an unprecedented form of empire abroad. Popular social science is read as contributing to meaning-making in a racialized and imperialized form of society. I conclude by considering how we might move beyond the dysfunctional politics and culture of scientism. In the past of the humanities lies the partial beginnings of a new, still unrealized future.

As should be abundantly clear, I am not chiefly concerned with the social scientific debates of higher academe. Rather, my focus is on how to read social science as a form of cultural creation and the popularization of social scientific authority in the popular realm of power and everyday practice. Although social science began life in a high, theoretical form written for other academics, the trajectory that interests me is downward into popular domains of debate not normally engaged by elite social scientific expert opinion. Such popularizations are rarely if ever read or taught in universities. But for better or worse they remain a chief conduit by which social science enters the culture and helps to build a much wider political world. Books of astonishing popularity with the general public, such as Steven Levitt and Stephen Dubner's *Freakonomics*, Malcolm Gladwell's *The Tipping Point*, and Steven Pinker's *How the Mind Works*, have helped shape the popular imagination and even build institutions and guide policy. Similar points could be made about works by academic social scientists who have defended their theories in popular forums, like James Q. Wilson's "Broken Windows" policing, Milton Friedman's championing of free markets, Samuel Huntington's clash of civilizations, and Francis Fukuyama's end-of-history thesis. I show how to read these and many other famous tracts of social science subversively, as forms of ideological creation and imagination.

The popularization of social science is thus central to my analysis. This means many of the social science texts I discuss—although often written by outstanding scholars in their respective fields, working at the most prestigious universities—are nevertheless not considered "real social science" by the standards of the scholarly community. I am aware that some social scientists, hastily perusing my book, might object: "But many of these theories are not actual social science. No one in academia takes these writings seriously!" And of course such a complaint contains a grain of truth, as many of the texts examined in these pages do not achieve the methodological rigor and complexity demanded by the genre of the scholarly monograph. So, for example, a political scientist reading my account of failed election forecasting might with some justification observe that many of the media forecasters were not actually political scientists. Moreover, as Nate Silver later noted, the polling from 2016 was neither more nor less accurate than past polling, and much of its overappraisal was generated in the realm of popular media.[2]

But in making this objection, the reader has conceded my starting point rather than refuted it—namely, that there exists a way of reading and writing social science that is paradoxically *not* chiefly scientific but rather cultural, political, and ideological. So the suggestion that the way I am reading and treating social science is not "authentic" or "correct" fails as an objection to my project, because the point is precisely to read social science with fresh eyes, not as a highly technical, descriptive discourse but as a way of exercising authority in society at large. Indeed, as the following chapters reveal, the line between the technical "high" versions of the social science genre and the "low" popularizations is not always so easily drawn. The problem of scientism—or an inflated, unwarranted confidence in the power of science to explain all of human life—exists both inside and outside the walls of the university campus.

But since I am pitting myself against the weight and authority of the word "science," I want from the outset to be perfectly clear about my intentions. My goal is emphatically not a critique of all social science or the value of the work of social scientists in general. On the contrary, there are thousands of social scientists engaged in noble, thoughtful, and deeply edifying work. As a society we need the information generated by social scientists, including mass polling, statistical regressions, interviewing, case studies, modeling, and ethnography. The work of the countless intelligent, creative, and insightful social scientists in our society is therefore to be valued and celebrated. Indeed, my own meditations in this book would not have been possible without the social scientific research of many scholars who have worked tirelessly in the pursuit of answering concrete questions about our shared social reality.

Neither is this book a rejection of the natural sciences. On the contrary, I am an admirer of what we call today the natural science revolution. But that natural science is among humanity's most startling accomplishments does not mean that all forms of knowledge ought to be crammed into its conceptual boxes, assumptions, and standards. The problem of scientism is that it is a very peculiar, modern type of superstition. How admiration of the natural sciences helps fuel its opposite (irrationalism and superstition) requires a bit more explanation.

Five hundred years ago one of the largest transformations in human history began, a movement that continues into the present day and whose scope is now global. This movement began in small pockets of Europe, led by clusters of intellectuals who called themselves "natural philosophers" and sought to recover ancient Greek and Roman sources. However, these thinkers quickly went beyond their ancient sources, devising new concepts, paradigms, and methods for studying the natural world. Soon they were upending everything that had been thought up to that time about the structure of the universe, the motion of objects, the anatomy of life, and the basic composition of reality. The result of their awe-inspiring intellectual creativity was a quantum leap forward in human understanding, which we now retrospectively call "the scientific revolution."

This revolution, moreover, is far from over. It is an intellectual movement whose advances many of the world's most powerful minds try to further and extend every day. This endeavor is one of the noblest undertakings of the human mind to date. It is a shared effort, which has come to span cultures, involving scientists from all over the globe of every conceivable race, creed, and nationality. It is also an intellectual movement with great beauty in its findings, delighting students, leaving many children hoping to grow old enough to understand better, and leaving many elderly people wishing they were children again to see what breakthroughs might come next.

Indeed, many modern people wear the scientific revolution like a badge of honor. These people sense that at least in this respect they are on the better side of a line dividing history. Why? Because although the knowledge acquired from the natural sciences is often put to abominable uses such as atom bombs and environmental degradation, these sciences have also undoubtedly improved human life in various indisputable ways. In applied form, the breakthroughs of the natural sciences have led to the soundest understanding of human physical well-being the world has known. Scientists have discovered practices to lengthen the average life span, medicines to cure once-devastating diseases, and therapies to diminish unnecessary pain and suffering.

The natural sciences have also laid the groundwork for innovations in technology that put all past civilizations in the shade—possibilities like routine flight, space exploration, and instant communication across enormous distances. The industrial and computer revolutions would have been impossible without the natural sciences, likewise the increased productivity of modern economies that has made supporting a larger population of human life possible. But even beyond all this (as any lover of the natural sciences will tell you), the study of the sciences is good for its own sake. It has revealed previously undreamt of mathematical and structural wonders—a world much stranger and more fascinating than any human mind had previously imagined. Many scientists affirm: the natural sciences are almost inexpressibly beautiful.

For all these reasons, I count myself among modern science's admirers and enthusiasts. However, all this justifiable enthusiasm for the natural sciences sometimes leads to a further and very different question, which is far more problematic. Might not the paradigm of the natural sciences be able to explain all of human life and reality? Might not a Newton of economics, a Copernicus of politics, and a Galileo of psychology be just around the corner? There is a widespread sense today that a second scientific revolution will complete the unfinished business of the first by explaining all of human life through science. When such a feat is finally accomplished, the sciences will be unified by a set of methods if not by an actual master, universal theory of everything. Then there will be no fundamental divide between the human sciences and the natural ones. At that point in time, British philosopher A. J. Ayer's famous call for a "unity of science" will finally be fulfilled, as will his view that "there is no field of experience which cannot, in principle, be brought under some form of scientific law, and no type of speculative knowledge about the world which it is, in principle, beyond the power of science to give."[3]

The payoffs of such a unification of the sciences, if it is ever achieved, would obviously be huge. Imagine if you had a scientific theory that predicted the outcome of elections (*you'd be powerful*), or a science of economics that allowed you to engineer human consumer behavior and incentives (*you'd be rich*), or a science of how to make great art by knowing what aesthetically stimulates the human brain (*you'd be famous*), or a science of what biologically makes human mates attractive (*you'd be desired*). There's only one problem with all this: there are very good reasons to believe that unifying all our understanding of the world under the banner of the natural sciences is impossible. Like medieval alchemists trying to turn base metals into gold, such a task may be impossible, not due to a lack of ingenuity or intelligence on the part of those working on the goal, but because the structure of reality itself does not permit it.

This brings me to the central philosophical perspective underlying my argument in these pages: the hermeneutic or interpretive outlook. Interpretive philosophy holds that achieving the unity of science is an impossible task because humans create and embody meanings in a way that requires the art of interpretation and not simply scientific explanation. In this view, human beings are fundamentally different within the order of things. As creative agents they continually spin new webs of meaning that form into practices, institutions, and the entire weave of social reality itself. Human social and political behavior does not fit under the conceptual logic of the natural sciences because it is not law-abiding or mechanistic in nature. The human sciences therefore have their own unique set of descriptive and explanatory concepts, and they are above all interpretive, humanistic disciplines, not formal, mechanistic ones.[4]

Consider, for example, the case of a lifelong registered Republican on Election Day 2016. No amount of demographic or other social scientific data (e.g., white, male, rural, evangelical) is enough to absolutely, securely determine or predict what his next action will be. Such an individual might interpret his beliefs in such a way that he comes to the conclusion that he could never vote for Trump (like the "never Trump" Republicans did), or he might instead reason in a way that makes voting for Trump vital to his sense of identity (the "Make America Great Again" voters). As a matter of fact, while standing in the ballot box, the very same individual might waiver back and forth between these two positions or any number of others creatively devised by his own reflections. To make an educated guess about what he will do next, we need an understanding of his life story, not a formal scientific prediction.

For those who prefer the precision of philosophical language to describe our Republican voter, in the case of human beliefs and actions, no set of antecedent conditions is ever sufficient to determine a consequent belief or action. This is in contrast to the natural sciences, in which antecedent conditions (all things being equal) can be used to predict a consequent condition or event. Therefore, no predictive science of human behavior is possible. Human actions simply do not embody the machine-like causality that is typical of Newtonian mechanics. Healthy human actions are never like the metallic "click" of a machine but are always contingent and can go very differently depending on how a given individual exercises his or her creative faculties. Just as no science will ever give you a plausible understanding of a Shakespeare play, so human behavior is only ultimately explicable through an art of interpretation.

This is also why interpretive philosophy maintains that the study of human behavior is one of the humanities and not a hard science. It is closer to the study of history or literature, because there is an analogy between studying texts and human beliefs and actions. Importantly, instead of relying on laws, explaining human actions requires telling particular stories or narratives about what has happened. Clearly telling stories or narratives dates back to human prehistory. This makes it much older than the scientific revolution. Some people are suspicious that stories or narratives are really the best we have when explaining human behavior. But if the interpretive position is true, then stories are simply the only rational way to explain human actions. The central task of the social sciences is therefore to tell the most objective, nuanced, complex, and true story about a given slice of social reality.

The primary story of this book is how social science, beginning as a high form of academic theory, can enter into the everyday world of ideology and culture and have unintended, sometimes even deeply sinister consequences that are obscured by a rhetoric of scientific neutrality and authority. Although this book focuses almost exclusively on how this has happened with social science theories, it can occur with theories in the natural sciences as well. For instance, one of the early breakthroughs in biology was the scientific classification of living organisms. A classic figure in this innovation was Carolus Linnaeus, the Swedish botanist and founder of the modern binomial system of taxonomy still employed by scientists. The binomial system joined two Latinate names, a generic genus and a particular species (e.g., *canis lupus* or *hydrangea macrophylla*), to rationally catalog a potentially indeterminate number of beings. This offered nothing less than a scientific method for naming all life on Earth.

However, Linnaeus's mania for scientific classification and its way of knowing the world also led him and his followers to extend such natural science categories beyond their rightful bounds. Historians have shown how Linnaeus, Georges-Louis Leclerc, Immanuel Kant, and other leading intellectuals of the Enlightenment implanted cultural, social, political, and other historical factors into supposed subcategories of *Homo sapiens* or the human species. This involved naturalizing into the anatomy of human beings what were not natural features at all but cultural perceptions and moral judgments, like "lazy," "avaricious," "acute," and "inventive." In doing so they built a pseudo-biological hierarchy that used cultural and moral qualities to demarcate subspecies, such as "White European," "Asiatic," "African," and "American" Indian. Thus, these leading minds of science and enlightenment actually helped invent the modern, pseudoscientific concept of race.[5]

Before the creation of such categories, people might have seen physical differences and felt a prejudice against them, but they would have had no conception of the reduction through science to a supposedly deeper hidden structure of biologically determined inferiority. Thus, in a very real sense modern racism only became possible when an abuse of natural science entered into our self-interpretations and social meanings. Although the idea that races were natural types failed as science, it succeeded in creating a new social and political world in which people perceived racial hierarchy as scientifically justified. Suddenly an experience that was impossible a century earlier became canonized by the power of the law and the state: a person's higher-order capacities and cultural identity were treated as biologically determined. First in Europe and later globally, people have been building pseudoscientific hierarchies of economy, theology, and politics based on a bogus "science" of racial classification ever since. Sometimes these efforts are defeated, but advocates of this form of power have also found new ways of expressing, justifying, and enacting their views. Indeed, as I show in chapter 5 on policing, such racial theories can receive subtle boosts and even entirely new architectures of power from supposedly neutral, scientific theories promulgated in the social sciences.

So efforts at descriptive scientific theory, when applied to human beings, can actually produce new identities, practices, and worlds of meaning. This is due to humans' uniquely creative meaning-making capacities and is what philosophers refer to as the "double hermeneutic effect," in which an interpretation of the world shapes the very interpretations that comprise it. Throughout the book I call these "double-H effects" for short.

Double-H effects make social science profoundly unlike the natural sciences, where the objects of study exist in a certain splendid seclusion and isolation. When a Ptolemaic astronomer places Earth at the center of the cosmos, the sun and the planets do not suddenly swivel violently, modifying their placement to match the theories on the page. Yet in the social sciences, the equivalent of Ptolemaic and Galilean astronomers change the basic social coordinates and field of objects with great frequency, in ways both intended and unintended by the theorists.

Much of this book is dedicated to identifying, diagnosing, and critically analyzing the social scientific double-H effects that created the world we currently inhabit. Viewed from the perspective of the double-H effect, much of social science (and particularly in its popular, vulgarized forms) is not simply descriptive but also performative. Social science as a genre can be read not in its official guise of neutral efforts at description but as artifacts of culture that participate in enacting and inaugurating certain political realities. I hope readers, once they view social scientific theories through these eyes, will be able to see that they are often slippery, escaping the hands of their creators and turning politically ambiguous, sometimes even menacing. This is to suggest nothing less than a form of power and politics completely unknown to epochs prior to the scientific revolution. Whereas the abuse of, say, religious or familial authority was well known to premoderns, the abuse of power by scientists or rather by scientism did not exist. And yet this frequently unrecognized form of domination pervades our societies.

Few people perceive this pervasive form of power, because scientism offers itself as the public, official, neutral, and objective way of doing things. Indeed, in extreme form scientism even tries to actively ban or eliminate other ways of knowing and experiencing the world as prescientific and illegitimate. The humanities, history, literature, the arts, philosophy, and religion are all disparaged as a kind of soft or even magical thinking. Even in mild forms, a culture of scientism subtly marginalizes the liberal arts and the humanities. Fewer people find it "useful" to study such things in college or fund them in primary schools, let alone name humanities scholars to positions of counsel in government and policy.

In the pages that follow, I uncover the hidden underbelly of a culture of scientism and reveal how what often presents itself as social science is instead culture and power. In doing so I seek to provoke readers to think carefully about the ways they themselves evoke the authority of science in everyday ethical and political life. Modern people must develop a critical sensibility for when science has flipped into a form of meaning-making with political and power dimensions flowing through it. Modern people must become critical readers of their own scientific cultures. This book is an effort to break out of the paradigm that holds us captive and tells us we are only allowed to read social science in one officially sanctioned manner.

Our rightful pride in the natural sciences has created a uniquely modern blind spot. In our quest to turn science into the measure of all things, we have generated a new kind of irrationality. Science becomes irrational when its ideal of knowledge is extended beyond its proper bounds and applied in areas where it does not rightfully hold sway. What is needed is a deeper awareness of the value of the humanities and the sensitive, interpretive intelligence required to grasp human life. Intellectually we still need to recover a profounder sense of our own—and others'—humanity.

PART I

The Market Polis

Our Free-Market Scientists

Before the housing bubble exploded in 2008—helping generate the largest financial crisis in a generation—anxious American homebuyers received a clear message from many professional economists: there was no housing bubble. For example, Chris Mayer and Todd Sinai (two Ivy League economists) wrote in 2005 in the *Wall Street Journal* that "economic logic" established the nonexistence of the bubble and that those who thought otherwise were economically illiterate "Chicken Littles."[1] Similarly, Gary Smith and Margaret Hwang Smith of Pomona authored a public policy piece in 2006 entitled "Bubble, Bubble, Where's the Housing Bubble?" In it they used economic models to argue that "the bubble is not . . . a bubble" and that "buying a house at current market prices" is an "attractive long-term investment."[2]

When the housing market finally crashed, vaporizing billions in real estate wealth, many ordinary Americans were forced to abandon not only their homes but also their feelings of financial security and self-worth. Indeed, many who experienced this loss had by 2016 slipped into a dark rage and social despair. These citizens learned bitter lessons about the financial crisis and the elites who had escaped it because the ruling powers deemed they were "too big to fail." *The system is rigged. Elites cannot be trusted. The world is filled with cheaters, and we must gather around an even bigger cheater to win. Someone or some group has sold out the republic.* Such lessons then helped fuel a collective search for scapegoats—racial, economic, ideological, and otherwise—a politics of rage that tore apart society in its efforts to restore it.

Economists in the popular arena often present themselves as a rational, scientific form of authority and economics as the standard-bearer for a bona fide science of human behavior. By contrast, the next two chapters consider how popular economic authorities have instead generated a number of unintended political and economic disasters that have radically altered the nature of democratic societies. Far from being a science, popular economic discourse has been closer to the fable of the sorcerer's apprentice, who under the illusion of mastery called forth powers he was unable to control. Claiming to have predictive knowledge and a science of prosperity, popular economists have often advocated behavior that has destroyed fortunes. Espousing equality and heightened access for all citizens, economic "science" in the last few decades has instead largely served as the basis for policies that have resulted in an ever-growing gap between the rich and the poor.

ECONOMICS AS POPULAR AUTHORITY

In the 1990s and early 2000s the prestige of economic intellectuals was at a cultural zenith in democratic societies. During this time economists held sway over an astonishing number of institutions, both public and private. Internationally, they had long controlled organizations such as the International Monetary Fund (IMF) and the World Bank; domestically, they ran most countries' monetary policies (in the United States alone they dominated the Federal Reserve, held a permanent advisory office in the White House, and staffed positions at all levels of government). Although economists were regularly thwarted in their policy goals, they nevertheless enjoyed unmatched power and influence compared to other social scientists and academics more generally. Indeed, scholars have established that the most pervasive way in which economists influenced the political world at that time was indirectly, through a "soft version of the economic style of reasoning" that had become increasingly ubiquitous among policy makers and the general public.[3]

Among other things, this economic style of reasoning supplied modern societies with a new conceptual vocabulary that transcribed the world of politics into economic categories. A few centuries earlier there had been no such discursive entity as "the economy" and thus no way to talk or think about it. But economists tirelessly worked to provide citizens with ostensibly neutral and quantifiable indicators such as stock and consumer indexes, gross domestic product (GDP), and the unemployment rate. These factors shaped public debate about an entity that had not existed in prior epochs but was now popularly referred to with the definite article: *the* economy. This grammatical construction communicated that the noun in question was already common knowledge, definite, objective, and universally valid. Everyone knew what *the* economy was and how to describe and measure it. An imagined entity and methodological fiction had achieved the same hardness as the now-permanent installation of street barricades around Congress and the White House.

A key feature in creating "the economy" as an object of collective contemplation was an elaborate statistics of economic indicators communicated via mass media. Where was the stock market index? What was the unemployment rate? What was the GDP per capita? Newspapers, television, and the Internet continually bombarded the public with these numbers as though they were simply offering a weather report. Many readers checked these reports ritualistically and compulsively (the German philosopher G. W. F. Hegel had long before noted that modern man prays over the newspaper), their eyes skimming over these indicators as if absorbing a secular horoscope. Individual well-being and social prosperity were carefully decrypted via this symbology.

Like the dashboard on a car, economic indicators allowed ordinary citizens to imagine an invisible engine vitally transporting society and all its members toward the goal of prosperity. What was rarely recognized was the fact that these indicators contained thousands of unseen choices and evaluations about what was socially and politically relevant and what was erasable from discussion. Persistent and entrenched poverty, for instance, did not figure prominently in the dominant scientific and descriptive indicators of this thing called "the economy"; neither did radically unequal access to the basic goods needed for human flourishing. The economy could therefore be healthy, roaring, and bullish, even as some citizens were permanently trapped in the pathologies of material want or other forms of economic malaise. The car was just fine so long as you didn't happen to live in the carburetor or exhaust pipe.

To speak of "the economy" during the 1990s and to control the narrative over what was happening to it became the central and at times only admissible domestic political conversation. One of the most famous political adages of the age was "it's the economy, stupid," a phrase coined by Bill Clinton's campaign adviser James Carville. Carville's quip implied that voters would ignore many political exigencies and travesties of justice but would not forgive indicators pointing to a weak economy. Political scientists had long debated whether economic indicators correlated with the outcomes of presidential elections.[4] Some popular forecasters, such as Yale economist Ray Fair, were favorites of the press because they were willing to adopt the simple claim that a critical mass of people voted on the basis of their "pocketbooks" and "how well off financially they expect to be in the future under each candidate."[5] As this social scientific literature descended into the everyday political world, correlation became causation, and common wisdom peddled in all the major newspapers held that "the economy" causally predicted and foretold campaign contests over the presidency.

Amid such wildly popular forecasting, no serious public debate was held about the possibility of a self-fulfilling, double-H effect, in which creating an electoral game around a scoreboard of very limited indicators (relying on one assemblage of accountancy measures to the exclusion of others) in turn inspired people to conform to this supposedly timeless electoral mechanics. Nor did a public discussion occur about the invention of a shared object (the economy) that would include some features of social reality while occluding or even erasing others.

Instead, throughout much of the 1990s intoning that "economics says this" or "such and such is good for markets" was in many circles an acceptable way to bring political debate to a grinding halt. Entire political traditions and ideological frameworks could be dismissed a priori as bad for the economy. Similarly, whole countries could be derided as not understanding economics and poorly managing their economies (a new version of the "civilization" versus "barbarism" split, intellectually laundered around economic jargon). Domestically, politicians and particularly U.S. presidents were increasingly assessed on how their tenures coincided with these scorekeeping measures, as if the public believed the presidential office had a set of wires and switches that were directly linked to the vital signs of the economy. And although no serious academic economist believed presidents alone could causally manipulate such features, the popularized "science" of economic indicators had escaped the hands of its academic creators and taken on nearly totemic qualities.

Of course many academic economists (although compulsively washing their hands of this sullied, vulgarized version of economics) nonetheless devised ways to benefit directly and indirectly from this public vaunting of economics into an oracular authority. Indeed, in academia economics had not coincidentally experienced a contemporaneous, astounding rise in fortunes both figurative and literal. Two centuries earlier economics had been a form of thinking inseparable from philosophy and history. The greatest economists of that earlier age had also been historians and political philosophers. But beginning in the twentieth century a new discipline of thought emerged that heavily stressed seemingly timeless formal models and mathematical sophistication. The historians, philosophers, and humanists were gradually kicked out of the respectable branches of the profession.

Economics began to adopt metaphors and techniques from engineering, mathematics, and the hard sciences. Economists spoke of equilibria, curves, coefficients, causal inferences, regressions, laws, and variables.[6] Banished from the mainstream of the discipline were ethical-political terms like exploitation, fairness, greed, and dignity. History and culture also disappeared from economics in favor of a kind of formalistic social physics. The pictures and models of economics had the appearance of existing in a perfect vacuum free of historical time and cultural space. As one historian of economics summarized this seismic intellectual shift, the new "quantitative techniques gave economics the aura of scientific modernity."[7]

This modern, mathematical, and scientific discipline of economics was also massively well funded. Universities and startling new crops of ideologized para-academies (referred to as "think tanks") received huge donations from corporate sponsors and public grants seeking to crack the secrets of the economy. As part of this trend, political elites and corporate chiefs began obsessing over a new economic construction: "*the* consumer." Market and political research sought to gauge and predict the behavior of this complex statistical aggregate. The consumer (as much an assemblage of facts as a person) was routinely interrogated via complex data and mathematical calculations, such as the consumer confidence index, said to help forecast savings and consumption trends. Political parties, businesses, corporations, and other organizations all sought to predict the behavior of this composite representative who was at once a social scientific everyman and a nobody.[8] As an elite politician one could rhetorically rule a democracy in the name of this imaginary person "the consumer" (along with the political science counterpart "the voter") and never actually grapple with the meanings and beliefs of particular persons by name. And as with the economy more generally, the consumer was also given the definite article in popular discourse. In an astonishing feat of imagination, millions of people knew exactly what was meant by *the* American consumer, though such a person did not exist except as an ideal imaginary of scientific fiction.

By the late twentieth century the new, more mathematically rigorous, and ahistorical form of economics had assumed pride of place on social science faculties. Economists' mathematical rigor and scientific sophistication made them in high demand in public policy and the private sector, which in turn enabled them to leverage their own expertise to claim that science itself dictated they receive higher salaries than their other colleagues in the liberal arts. As one university dean, reflecting on the consistently large pay gap between economists and humanities scholars, confessed in 2002: "There's no question that chairs of economics departments understand market forces better than other chairs."[9]

The economy's supply and demand curves—and all the impersonality and inexorability these entailed—simply demonstrated that economists were scientifically more deserving of higher pay. A claim of merit and just deserts took on the appearance of a value-neutral, descriptive fact. Such dynamics might be considered an especially intense version of a double-H effect, in which social scientific theories already embodied in everyday culture are extracted and retheorized by economists and taken as confirmation of their original theories.

Economists could even claim to be the sole social scientists to have their own Nobel Prize. Could anyone seriously doubt that economics was an objective science? Other social science disciplines were racing to incorporate economic theories of rational choice and econometric-style statistics; political science, sociology, psychology, and even evolutionary biology all had their economized wings. If physics set the standard of science for research into the natural world, economics now did the same for the social domain.

Beginning in the 1970s the increasingly laissez-faire tendencies that informed much of popular economic theory were catechized into entire generational cohorts of undergraduates and other novice students, disseminated via programs in economics, accounting, and business (the latter consistently remaining the country's most popular field of study in higher education). In this way, an entire generation of college graduates in America was socialized into the notion that the formal, mechanical dynamics of markets represented a leading-edge science and that this science was in no way morally, politically, or ideologically biased. Like all true sciences, it was timeless, mechanical, and immaculate.

Average citizens outside the walls of academe increasingly sought out and followed the directives of popularized, free-market economic science. One of the most influential political and policy magazines of that era was simply dubbed *The Economist*. Millions of readers likewise turned simplifications of economic theory such as Steven Levitt and Stephen Dubner's *Freakonomics* or Tyler Cowen and Alexander Tabarrok's *Marginal Revolution* into massive cultural phenomena. In this vulgarized form, free-market economics was said to explain everything about human behavior—not just consumer choices but also romance, crime, education, naming practices, organ donation, aesthetics, family well-being, philanthropy, scientific research, novel reading, tech innovation, nutrition, sumo wrestling, abortion, and the Ku

Klux Klan. Economics simply was (as the subtitle to Levitt and Dubner's astonishingly popular book stated) the scientific explanation of "everything."

Economics was queen, and at a time when American sentiments about intellectuals in universities were at a remarkably low ebb, this class of scholars was instead vested with special status (though only if they conformed to the popular orthodoxy). Of course, economists inside the walls of academia rarely shared or endorsed the simplistic conception of their own discipline presented by the likes of Levitt, Dubner, Cowen, and Tabarrok. They were more cautious about the fact that their models were just that: simplifications, thought experiments, and game scenarios that might sometimes shed light on a very narrow range of human activities restricted to the production, trade, and consumption of material goods. Such economists did not dare claim that they practiced an indubitable science of society, let alone held the master key for unlocking the secrets of human behavior in all domains of life. Yet this was not the form of economics that had triumphed in the popular imagination.

Crucial to the authority of this popular "science" of economics was its claim not merely to describe but also to scientifically predict the dynamics of the economy. Whereas historians and other humanities scholars were restricted in their relevance to arcane knowledge of the human past that generated little or no material wealth, popular economists promised scientific knowledge of a future of prosperity and innovation. This followed the argument made by one of the most publicly influential economists of the late twentieth century, Milton Friedman. A Noble laureate and key figure in the Chicago School of economics, Friedman conceded that economic models were empirically distorted (perhaps even false) abstractions. Nonetheless, he insisted that these economic models had the power to predict future outcomes.

In his widely read 1953 essay, "The Methodology of Positive Economics," Friedman drew an analogy between economic science and physics. Both forms of research, Friedman noted, constructed idealized models; in physics material bodies fell through perfect vacuums, while in economics actors rationally calculated on the basis of perfect information. Friedman inferred from this analogy that neither physics nor economics rested on the realism of its theoretical assumptions. And if physics, often recognized as the standard-bearer in the natural sciences, was based on unrealistic constructions, then economics' apparent disconnect from empirical reality might also be justified. Friedman dramatically concluded: "The relevant question to ask about the 'assumptions' of a theory is not whether they are descriptively 'realistic,' for they never are"; rather, the essential question is whether they yield "sufficiently accurate predictions."[10] The counterintuitive upshot of Friedman's argument (echoed by countless economists ever since) was that empirically distorted and even false assumptions might still generate scientifically predictive knowledge.

Subsequent testing of Friedman's proposal, however, proved fundamentally problematic. Indeed, economists never made good on acquiring predictive powers that exceeded educated guesswork (let alone powers approaching those of physics and the other natural sciences). Perhaps the most comprehensive empirical evidence to date established that economic experts are unable to outperform amateurs in predicting a wide range of economic indicators, including GDP growth, unemployment, and inflation.[11] The main researcher behind these findings, Philip

Tetlock, came to the following unsettling conclusion: "People who devoted years of arduous study to a topic were as hard-pressed as colleagues casually dropping in from other fields to affix realistic probabilities to possible futures."[12] In fact, economic experts did not even manage to outdo computers that were running on "crude extrapolation algorithms," let alone "sophisticated statistical ones."[13]

Yet the fact that economists were unable to predict the future better than anybody else even when narrowly limited to market transactions (and excluding the complexities of human behavior more generally) did not diminish the influence of popular, free-market "science." Instead, free-market economists continued to enjoy pride of place in both the public and private sectors, wielding a hugely disproportionate influence over policy. In other words, although Friedman's rhetorical strategy of transferring the prestige and authority of physics onto economics proved a failure philosophically, it became a spectacular success ideologically. Friedman's defense of economics did not stand on its own terms, but his basic rationale did form a lasting apologetics for popular economic authority. In this way, popular economic authority was rhetorically and politically enacted, not scientifically achieved.

THE SPONTANEOUS-MACHINE METAPHOR AND ITS MALFUNCTIONS

Certainly what Tetlock uncovered as true of economic expertise in general was evident in the particular case of the 2008 recession. Few economic experts foresaw the worst recession in a generation, and even among the handful that noted troubling signs, none commanded the replicable, scientific ability to predict the future. Yet though it lacked a predictive theory of major economic events such as the 2008 crisis, economics did have the power to help create them. Popular economics as a form of mass culture had in fact played a key role in engendering the recession and a widening inequality. This point requires some explaining.

One important way that economic expertise could turn into mass culture was through the deployment of metaphors said to capture technical, scientific insight. The metaphor of the market as a spontaneous machine that automatically self-corrected was particularly important in this regard. This metaphor had a long history, dating back several centuries to the early Enlightenment. Deistic thinkers during this time had viewed both nature and society as a machine without an intentional designer (i.e., God). For example, Adam Smith had famously imagined "every individual" as "continually exerting himself" to find out "his own advantage," and although "he intends only his own gain," he is guided as if by "an invisible hand" to "promote the public interest."[14]

Smith's "invisible hand" was a metaphor for a spontaneous social mechanics, which although lacking a designer, paradoxically took on the best economic design possible. Unlike traditional Christian theism, which taught that individuals must radically convert into a new moral life, Smith maintained that this spontaneous mechanics began from individuals remaining self-interested and morally unchanged. Indeed, Smith argued that when it came to trade, the general material prosperity of all was best served by individual self-interest and the noninterference of government. Thus, in its most basic form, the spontaneous-machine metaphor expressed by Smith held that the economy was a design without a designer, the natural result of self-interested individuals freely pursuing their own material well-being.

In the twentieth century, Friedrich Hayek further elaborated upon the metaphor of society as a benevolent, spontaneous machine. Despite having won a Nobel Prize in economics, Hayek was largely kept on the fringes of academic economics for a perceived lack of analytical rigor. Whatever he may have lacked in mathematical virtuosity, he far outmatched his peers in a talent for imaginatively evoking certain assumptions behind the technical models and giving them an explicitly ideological bent (inevitably against social democracy and in favor of free markets). Hayek thus found his most enduring readership outside of academia and among politicians and lay readers seeking to remake society on a laissez-faire model.

In one of his seminal writings, Hayek explained that a market system was a "marvel" rivaling "the greatest triumphs of the human mind," because although it was "not the product of human design," it nonetheless organized knowledge and scarce resources optimally and enabled individuals to "take the right action." Indeed, Hayek insisted it was "more than a metaphor" to describe the completely unplanned, undesigned free-market system "as a kind of machinery."[15] Hayek believed that relevant economic information was spontaneously distributed across the economy in a way that maintained individuals in a maximally rational and free condition. There were therefore moral and not just material reasons to favor a laissez-faire economy.

The many differences between Smith and Hayek notwithstanding, the popular economic metaphor of the spontaneous machine did much to help conjure economic authority as rational and scientific in the public mind. Indeed, if society was a spontaneous machine, then surely economics was a scientific manual, guiding individuals in how to make this machine work properly. Moreover, this economic metaphor seemed to offer a simple political moral: government was bad at organizing, while this spontaneous thing called the economy was sleek and good at it. Paradoxically, this would mean economists and government would need to intervene to create laissez-faire markets and break up all associations seen as creating frictions in the machine (e.g., unions, city governments, local trade practices, left-wing ideologies). Constant intervention in democratic life, majority decisions, laws, and associations were all justified in the name of the underlying spontaneous machine.

Following a version of this spontaneous-machine metaphor, much of the popular economic authority that reigned prior to the 2008 recession pointed in the direction of continual deregulation of markets, including repealing legal restrictions on risks taken by lending banks as well as eliminating any checks on complex financial products such as derivatives. In a metaphor imagined by millions of people simultaneously, markets were a bundle of self-correcting forces. They reached equilibriums, responded to failures, and aggregated information in a manner far superior to any conscious effort of the human mind. As Hayek had said, perhaps humankind's best machine was an accidental invention or no real invention at all but rather a spontaneously occurring order.

This metaphor loomed large behind the popular economic authorities who counseled ordinary Americans that there was no housing bubble and that they should continue investing in houses. After all, destructive disequilibria were the result of government policy and never of individual, self-interested actions. The possibility that instead of benevolent outcomes, individual market actors might unwittingly create a societal crisis (a housing glut, unpayable loans, toxic assets, etc.) was literally unimaginable according to the basic metaphor. Indeed, Hayek had taught that markets spontaneously stabilized around prices, which implied that in the price of a home an individual had most of the information he or she needed to make a rational, socially beneficial choice while maximizing his or her personal interests.

What popular, free-market economists rarely if ever considered during this period was the possibility that the metaphor of a spontaneous-machine society might be helping to create the very thing the metaphor denied—namely, market-driven economic disasters. To those who believed in the technical models underlying the simplified metaphor, such outcomes were excluded by a highly rigorous science that made certain idealized assumptions about human rationality. The idealized models predictably showed that such things could not occur. In this way, a certain strain of popular economic authority made it difficult for many people to imagine the very phenomenon that this mode of idealized thinking helped spawn.

Such a conclusion is corroborated by the "Dahlem Report," produced by a small group of dissenting economists who published a sharp rebuke of the profession in the wake of the financial crisis. In it they argued that modern economics had become captive to highly mathematized models and idealized conceptions of individual rational self-interest that eclipsed the real world. The precision of the mathematical models fed an illusion of scientificity and predictive powers among both economists and the general public. And this abstract, idealized formalism, the Dahlem Report concluded, was also linked to an enormous and unfounded faith in free markets as spontaneously stable and rational orders.[16]

In short, economic theory led to unforeseen, self-defeating consequences. Promising a science of wealth creation, it jumped the boundaries of respectable academic discourse and became a vulgarized, simplistic metaphor that helped justify a massive, collective act of wealth destruction. To make matters worse, creating such free markets had been a carefully planned political project conducted over several generations; the ensuing wealth destruction had been planned by no one. The metaphor of a benevolent, spontaneous machine therefore was generating a deep form of confusion and malfunction.

But such confusion also led to unintended ethical and political consequences. Although professional economists often drew a bright line between science and advocacy, in the popular realm economic science in these decades was frequently said to be on the side of individual freedom, increased prosperity, and equality. The example of school vouchers illustrates how this led to self-defeating ethical and political outcomes. The parties and advocates of individual freedom and choice often in practice eroded the conditions for the possibility of exercising individual free agency.

In the late twentieth century there was a mass-mobilized, bipartisan effort to quasi-privatize America's school systems through the establishment of charter schools and vouchers. This political project had received a key early articulation by Milton Friedman in his 1955 essay, "The Role of Government in Education." There Friedman argued that one way to reorganize public schools along the spontaneous, benevolent features of markets would be to provide parents with "vouchers" or a portable form of funding that would be assigned to the schools of their choice. In this way, parents and students would become shoppers, and schools would be more like entrepreneurs, trying to attract the largest share of students or customers with their product. As Friedman put it, "here, as in other fields, competitive private enterprise is likely to be far more efficient in meeting consumer demands than . . . nationalized enterprises."[17] Transforming public schools into a spontaneous-market system would, according to Friedman, have the predictable effect of widening "the range of choice available to parents" and "equalizing opportunity" in a way that public schools were incapable of achieving.[18]

Friedman's proposal for vouchers and a competitive market environment of charter and public schools was implemented piecemeal over the course of several decades. A culminating triumph in this movement was Donald Trump's appointment of a zealous advocate of voucherized schools (Betsy DeVos) as his secretary of education. DeVos had long argued that government-run schools were a monopoly and therefore cumbersome and un-innovative. By contrast, marketizing the public system by introducing vouchers and making public schools compete with charter and even private schools would predictably bring with it a creative energy akin to that of the Silicon Valley's tech explosion. "As long as education remains a closed system," she forecasted, "we will never see the education equivalents of Google, Facebook, Amazon, PayPal, Wikipedia, or Uber."[19]

Looming behind such thinking was the spontaneous-machine metaphor that held that individuals acting in their own self-interest created benevolent social outcomes. Before assuming her national post, DeVos had already had a large influence in introducing vouchers and school choice in Detroit, which in part due to her efforts had adopted these policies earlier than other cities. Although advocates for this marketization of school systems (from Friedman to DeVos) stressed the equalizing effects of such policy, Detroit had experienced the exact reverse. In the wake of vouchers and school choice, investigative reporting uncovered massive differential outcomes in Detroit's school system for the poor versus the rich. Among the consequences was increased defunding or closing of schools in poorer districts deemed unable to compete by supposed market measures such as ability to attract students (customers) or raise standardized test scores (efficient output). The result was that some poor areas of Detroit had effectively become educational deserts, from which parents might need to travel many miles to take their children to school.[20] A movement for individual choice and enhanced educational quality had ended up undermining the ability of poor Detroiters to accomplish either.

At the same time, vouchers had successfully funneled money toward wealthy districts, where parents were able to present their existent privilege as greater objective merit and market competitiveness. Indeed, charter schools in rich districts could show that they were objectively more efficient by the standards of free-market economic science and standardized test scores. They could also attract greater numbers of student-customers from those families who had the relevant information and were financially able to make the sacrifices and requisite efforts to coordinate better schooling for their children. Indeed, in places like Los Angeles Unified School District, where a hugely complex and highly unequal system of private, charter, and magnate schools had formed, wealthier parents even began to hire admissions consultants, who helped them to apply to the best schools and maximize benefits for their children. Rather than a rational market of equal choosers, school choice had spawned a labyrinth of public goods wherein benefits were informally funneled through increasingly obscure mechanisms toward those who had the greatest resources and away from the poor.

Rationally, fully informed choices were only possible for those who could afford to reflect on a plan and enjoyed the means to execute it. The result was rampant inequality. Nevada introduced a school choice policy in 2015 that was used by the wealthiest residents of Reno and Las Vegas to concentrate state funding at the top of the economic ladder.[21] In this way, the metaphor of a spontaneous market machine had in practice served for state intervention to redistribute money upward away from the poor and toward the rich. Market competition had generated its winners and its losers. School choice and vouchers had fed a dynamic in which low-performing communities were increasingly defunded as "losers" of economic innovation, while wealthy high performers were given more and more funding on the grounds that the market had dictated this outcome.

All of this was exactly the opposite effect of what Friedman had predicted when he claimed that under vouchers American schools would experience greater equality, and parents would not "flock together," preventing "a healthy intermingling of children from decidedly different backgrounds."[22] Friedman (who placed enormous stock in economics' predictive powers) had forecast the exact reverse effects for his voucher plan. The spontaneous machine of the market had malfunctioned. In one sobering example, Friedman's claims to have predictive, scientific powers and to be a crusader in the cause of advancing individual freedom and equality had both been contradicted.

Where Friedman did succeed was in teaching millions of his readers to view the idealized, frictionless models of economics as if they were the mechanics of Newtonian physics. In the models, vouchers as a vehicle to liberty and equality had perhaps not yet been disproven. All that was needed was the ingenuity to reinterpret reality to fit the metaphor. Indeed, the popular metaphor of a spontaneous machine (supposedly backed by a highly technical, mathematized economic science) might yet create a profound restructuring of society according to the dictates of laissez-faire. This creation of an utterly new form of free-market republic—based on a popularized conception of economic life—is my next topic.

Republic Inc.

The 2008 financial collapse resulted from the intoxicating pursuit of self-interest at the expense of the public good. Lawmakers deregulated financial markets to please Wall Street donors, Wall Street traded toxic assets for quick profits, regulators inflated grades on these toxic loans to avoid upsetting their customers, homebuyers took out toxic loans they could not repay to buy dream houses; and realtors and developers sold houses to people who ultimately could not afford them. This grand carousel of greed was all accompanied by the a cappella music of politicians, newspapers, and popular economists singing about the virtues of American homeownership.

How did American society come to be populated by so many craven egoists? One venerable answer, originating with Aristotle, suggests that the spread of such a mentality in society reflects a faulty moral and political education. The economic crisis, in other words, began as a crisis in education. This requires a little background.

Aristotle argued in his *Nicomachean Ethics* that a just citizen needed to be taught from a young age to cultivate virtues like justice, moderation, and prudence and to eliminate vices like profligacy, overindulgence, greed, and vanity. Failure to habituate to these virtues and integrate them deep into one's character would lead to a citizenry willing to pillage society and the public good for the sake of their own private profit. Were Americans taught certain subliminal moral messages by popular economics and social science?

One point that is indisputable is that mainstream, academic economics had long before shelved Aristotle's ethical analysis of human actions as insufficiently scientific. The academic discipline of economics taught that no ethical or ideological judgments could ever enter into a bona fide, descriptive science. Moreover, descriptive economic science started from the unsentimental principle that all humans were self-interested preference maximizers. Thus, although the 2008 crisis might have been avoided by revamping institutions and incentive structures, the human species could no more be expected to abandon calculative self-interest than to transform from bipeds into centipedes.

In what follows I suggest that a popularized, mass form of free-market economic theory helped create the culture of egoism that fed into the 2008 crisis. This constitutes nothing less than a massive double-H effect. Specifically, beginning in the later part of the twentieth century, millions of people learned to interpret themselves as preference maximizers or an extreme version of what philosophers call *Homo economicus* (economic man). This vision of human life was never simply a scientific theory existing on the page, but rather played a key role in the radical reshaping of modern democracies and can even be linked to later backsliding away from traditions of democratic, popular rule.

BUILDING ECONOMIC MAN

Imagining *Homo economicus* was always part of building him. The earliest efforts to envision humans as naturally haggling, materially acquisitive, and self-interested had roots in Europe. In 1689 John Locke published a classic articulation of this view in his *Second Treatise of Government*. Locke was among the first to imagine humans in their supposedly primitive and natural state as proto-capitalists, trucking and bartering goods they had eked out of nature. For Locke, aboriginal man existed self-reliantly in the wilderness, gathering bushels of apples, acorns, plums, and other sundry goods for occasional barter. As he put it, humans before the advent of government traded "nuts for a piece of metal . . . sheep for shells."[1] In this supposedly natural state, humans had no religious, tribal, or group identity of any kind. Politics and culture did not exist. Rather, humankind's principal concern was materialistic: acquisition, industry, and individual survival.

Thus, Locke was among the first to justify capitalism by imagining a form of society that had never existed before: a loose economic network of self-reliant hagglers. Readers of Locke's "state of nature" theory were asked to make an imaginative leap and picture themselves in a way that would have been impossible for, say, medieval peasants or lords to comprehend three centuries earlier. In doing so Locke became one of the key founders of the concept of *Homo economicus*. Yet in stark contrast to later advocates of this view, Locke did not suggest that human society could exist on this economic basis alone. On the contrary, Locke believed that no society could consist of negotiation and self-interest alone; humans needed to engage and cultivate their sociable sentiments.

Surprising to many contemporary readers is the fact that Locke argued that humans in nature recognized a just limit on the accumulation of private property. Specifically, natural right held that no more could be taken out of the commons than one could use without it spoiling; moreover, enough had to be left within nature for others to subsist. Locke therefore believed that humans had a kind of universal right to make a living. On this last point Locke was clear: he who "took more than his share . . . robbed others."[2]

Similarly, another key champion of early *Homo economicus*, Adam Smith, maintained that a society of economic interests must be balanced by sentiments of solidarity. Indeed, Smith did not believe that economic interests alone could sustain social life; instead, members of society needed to care for those who were suffering hardships, illness, and economic want. Especially important was a sentiment Smith called "fellow feeling," which allowed individuals to sympathize with the misfortunes of "every man, merely because he is our fellow creature."[3] Smith suggested that without fellow-feeling, a society of mere economic interests would fall into a deep malaise and even collapse.

The early version of *Homo economicus* was therefore moderate compared with later slogans popularized by the likes of Ayn Rand's disciples, who believed that greed was good and that egoism was a key feature of the movers and builders of industrial society. This far more radical view of *Homo economicus* emerged closer to our own time, when free-market economists jettisoned Locke's state of nature and Smith's notion of human sentiments as insufficiently scientific. In their place they adopted a highly technical theory of human behavior that assumed all actions were motivated by self-interest. The most sophisticated form of this theory was called "rational choice" and was gradually employed across the social sciences.[4] Based on a few logical assumptions, rational choice pictures individuals as relentlessly preference maximizing. Although very far from representing the whole of economics, this theory represented the most analytically rigorous version of *Homo economicus*.

At the simplest level, rational choice constructs an ideally rational agent by formulating basic principles or axioms said to be characteristic of individuals in decision-making scenarios. While rational choice theorists have hypothesized a number of axioms, two are crucial: completeness and transitivity.[5] The completeness axiom holds that rational individuals can rank all preferences (indifference and ties are allowed), while transitivity says individual preferences are transferable and noncircular (e.g., a person who prefers beer to wine and wine to champagne also prefers beer to champagne).

Rational choice taken as a form of *Homo economicus* offers a vision of humans as constantly strategizing how to best satisfy their preferences. All human beliefs and actions are transcribed into the same formal logic; this enables economists to build models of idealized decision-making scenarios. It also allows them to treat all human goals (from altruism to bald-faced profit making) as just alternative options in a preference schedule. Once placed in the context of a rational choice model, those selecting altruistic goals appear to be no less self-interested and calculating than anybody else. Indeed, in this view, altruists simply happen to prefer moral feelings, honor, or whatever other profit they gain from empathizing with others. Working in finance or feeding the poor in a soup kitchen are thus both rendered rationally egoistic.

Within the wider culture of scientism, there is a complex relationship between the credibility of the highly technical, mathematical forms of rational choice and popular economic rhetoric about human life. While most academic economists understand that rational choice theory is an idealized model with very narrow applications, an influential cadre of popular economists sometimes slips into presenting this vision of human life as central to a "decision science." For these rogue economists the account of human behavior offered by rational choice is not simply an idealized thought experiment but a science that describes and predicts how humans reason and act in the world. In other words, the logic of preference maximizing is said to unveil a deep truth about human nature as being essentially economic.

A key figure in this popularizing move was economist and Nobel laureate Gary Becker, who believed economics had uncovered nothing less than a "unified framework for understanding all human behavior."[6] According to Becker, the crucial insight of economics was a logic or structure of choice in which humans consistently ranked and sought to maximize their individual consumption preferences. Beginning in the late 1960s, Becker thus influentially advocated for applying what he called the "economic approach" far outside the boundaries of traditional economics, to explain everything from marriage rituals to crime patterns. Admirers of Becker, University of Chicago economist Steven Levitt and journalist Stephen Dubner turned this imperial conception of economics (as the reigning discipline of the social sciences) into the *Freakonomics* series of books and media, which became in the early aughts the most popular economics phenomenon for an entire generation.

Free of the dry technicalities of rational choice theory, *Freakonomics* taught a simplified version of its basic tenets, depicting human reasoning as reducible to a consistent structure of strategic choice and incentives. Millions of readers learned how to imagine themselves, their actions, and their world in light of this basic logic of incentives. According to Levitt and Dubner, everything from how to raise children to Japanese sumo wrestling was explicable as the calculations of *Homo economicus*. Levitt and Dubner even declared that the economic science of incentives uncovered the "hidden side of everything." Self-interest was thus not socially destructive or greedy but simply the rational, inescapable way of being human. "The act of altruism is not as pure as it might appear," Levitt and Dubner warned their readers as they catechized them into the basics of economic science.[7]

A mere three years before the 2008 financial meltdown, Levitt and Dubner argued in their most popular book that real estate agents who self-interestedly cheated clients out of the most competitive prices for their homes were simply being rational. Levitt and Dubner made this case by citing statistical data showing that a significant percentage of real estate agents in the United States sold their own properties at higher rates than those of their clients. They then proceeded to argue that a science of choice explained why this was a predictable, even inevitable result. This was because agents at that time received 1.5 percent of the purchase price on a residential property. Therefore a hefty difference of $10,000 in home price for a client was only a measly $150 for the agent. In other words, realtors rationally ranking their preferences had no compelling incentive to work harder for their clients only to earn such a small differential. With such an incentive structure in place, the science of economics determined that realtors would predictably expend more effort to secure the best deals on their own homes rather than on those of their clients.

Levitt and Dubner presented these conclusions in the dispassionate, objective voice of science. Realtors who consistently fetched worse deals for their clients than for themselves were in no way egoistic, greedy, lacking empathy, or otherwise shirking their moral obligation to their clients. "The point here is not that real estate agents are bad people," they wrote, "but simply that they are people—and people inevitably respond to incentives."[8]

Although Levitt and Dubner did not know it at the time, thousands of real-life realtors, along with investors, politicians, lenders, developers, and consumers, were carrying out precisely this kind of shortsighted and materially acquisitive calculus, to disastrous effect. And though Levitt and Dubner never predicted the biggest economic event of their lifetimes, they did play a role in the culture of egoism that created it. Indeed, a follower of the *Freakonomics* sensation in the early 2000s would have learned that calculating in terms of rational self-gain at the cost of others was simply the scientific thing to do.

Thus, what *Freakonomics* communicated to huge numbers of readers was a highly vulgarized, simplified version of academic economics that cheerfully borrowed from the latter's reputation for scientific authority to advance its own status and agenda. In this way, a popular economic science teaching the inescapability of egocentrism gained all the inevitability of astronomy and heliocentrism. The rationally calculative actor was at the center of the social world, just as the sun was at the center of the solar system, and no amount of moral kvetching or philosophizing could make it otherwise.

Freakonomics was therefore one very visible instance of a far wider cultural revolution and double-H effect. This involved the creation of nothing less than a new meaning of citizenship in democratic societies—one that jettisoned Locke's and Smith's concern with sentiments of social solidarity while radicalizing a notion of haggling self-interest. The supposed science of economics had encouraged citizens to transform themselves from empathetic members of the same community (with fellow feeling for all of humankind) into "rational" economic consumers passing unceasingly through an endless series of market scenarios. A form of ethical, cultural, and political production claimed the mantel of scientific authority.

A few sensitive social observers had noticed this troubling cultural revolution in democratic societies over a decade earlier. In the 1990s, the psychologist Philip Cushman had reported increasing cases of a new kind of "empty," consumer self showing up in clinical practice. This self viewed all social relations as economic, market relations and all personal problems as surmountable by consuming the right products and achieving a desired lifestyle, advertised in celebrity culture.[9] For this kind of self, even deeply personal relationships were essentially negotiated consumption choices. Marriages, families, friendships, workplaces, schools, churches, and governments were all sites of self-interested consumer calculations. Indeed, there was no such thing as a shared school, family, or civic interest. Instead, everything was subsumable under the metaphor of loose networks of individuals vying for their uppermost preference. This is one way of understanding the recent ubiquity of market talk and market metaphors in society. For example, the latter is evidenced in Jared Kushner's public proclamations that his wife Ivanka Trump "is definitely the CEO of our household, whereas I'm more on the board of directors."[10] For *Homo economicus*, even the family is a business.

Likewise, American sociologist Robert Bellah had warned several decades earlier about a radical change in how ordinary people were conceiving of their social lives. According to Bellah's analysis, based on a large number of detailed interviews, a radically autonomous, atomized individual was emerging, disconnected from surrounding personal and civic associations. In romantic relations Bellah noted a hyper-individualistic mentality among couples, in which autonomy and the ability to choose other options at all times was paramount. This autonomous self also viewed love as a kind of subjective consumer preference based on no other justification than that it "feels right."[11] Individuals only exercised rationality in ranking preferences and retaining the ability to choose, not in a substantive capacity to encounter deep meanings (a point I return to in detail in a later chapter).

In this way, mass culture increasingly imitated a vulgar version of the scientific logic of high economic theory (albeit always in highly distorted form). What emerged was an extended metaphor of society as an individualistic market. Society itself was simply a relationship between producers and consumers. The right to exit such a society and its duties—for example, if Silicon Valley executives had the means to move to other countries to avoid high tax rates—was merely an economic calculation like any other (e.g., buying bananas at the store) and not a betrayal of patriotism or majority sovereignty in a democracy. Similar claims could be made about avoiding military and civil service or otherwise shirking traditional roles of citizenship. In fact, cheating the common good simply made one rational and clever (not paying taxes made one "smart"). After all, there was no public good once the assumptions of a decision science were in place. Rather, the whole point of society was to acquire the best "deal" possible for oneself personally. This brings us to the birth of the market polis.

THE MARKET POLIS

The market polis is a political society in which all relationships and institutions are transcribed into a metaphor of self-interested deal making and whose authority is said to derive from economic science. In a market polis everyone—from the highest political officeholder to the ordinary citizen on the street—is a rational-choice actor, shrewdly calculating in order to maximize personal preferences. In the social sciences, the market polis has found expression beyond economics in disciplines from psychology to political science.

One widely influential political scientist who reimagined politics as a self-interested market was the congressional scholar David Mayhew.[12] Mayhew's 1974 book, *Congress: The Electoral Connection*, became a classic in contemporary political science by arguing that legislative actors behaved according to the logic of rational choice, rendering them essentially careerists seeking to retain office. "In the fashion of economics," Mayhew wrote, "I shall make a simple abstract assumption about human motivation. . . . I shall conjure up a vision of United States congressmen as single-minded seekers of reelection."[13]

What Mayhew's shift in paradigm purportedly revealed was that America's legislators were exclusively engaged in one of three activities intended to help them win elections: advertising their accomplishments, taking credit for policy outcomes, and ostentatiously adopting electorally popular positions. Mayhew claimed his theory was strictly "scientific."[14] But like Becker and Levitt, he in fact offered a radically new vision of individuals who lacked any sentiments of empathy, fellow feeling, or social solidarity. Or rather, such sentiments were just one more item in a self-interested bid to maximize a hierarchy of preferences, with election to office and a congressional career sitting at the tiptop. This meant that in effect the highest lawmakers in the land were no different than real estate agents, and to ask for virtuous, public-minded legislators was unreasonable because it misunderstood political science.

Mayhew was following a much larger reimagining of society, which borrowed from the authority of economics to supposedly lay bare the mechanics of human action. Another key figure in this trend was the Nobel Prize–winning economist, James Buchanan. Buchanan deployed *Homo economicus* assumptions to argue that civil servants and bureaucrats necessarily had self-interested incentives to balloon government programs and budgets.[15] Working without market competition, civil servants (i.e., everyone from postal workers to military leaders) would seek to grow their fiefs at the expense of the taxpayer. Buchanan therefore advised that public institutions should be privatized or contracted out to entrepreneurs.

Social science therefore imagined a radically new polis in the name of simply describing it. Like Mayhew's political science, Buchanan's economic science allowed for no meaningful difference in the motivations of a patriotic civil servant and a private sector contractor. Both were fundamentally seeking to maximize personal profit. Buchanan did not hesitate to use the authority of science to bolster his conclusions. He insisted that his findings were ideologically neutral "science," and that there was

no fundamental difference between his work and that of a "physical scientist" making "progress toward uncovering the laws that
govern" the world.[16]

Yet such "scientific" findings were never fully separable from
the demand to remake government. Indeed, drawing on this social scientific literature, many politicians and ordinary citizens
began calling for all major institutions of society to be remodeled
as businesses. The description subtly implied prescriptions.
Common policy dictates included rolling back government
programs; introducing economic austerity; privatizing goods and
services; and subjecting employees to various incentive schemes,
measured outcomes, and assessment, said to render the work
environment more like an efficient market. Together with the
changing cultural conceptions of selfhood and citizenship understood as an extreme form of *Homo economicus*, these policies
helped institutionally build a market polis for people to inhabit.

The global ascendancy of the market polis reached the highest
halls of power with the elections of Margaret Thatcher in Great
Britain in 1979 and Ronald Reagan in the United States in 1980.
Reagan's popular attacks on the culture of solidarity were so
transformative that during the 1990s and early 2000s, leaders
in the highest ranks of both political parties effectively adopted
his vision of the state as an inefficient, poorly run business. So
in the years that followed the "Reagan Revolution," Democratic
president Bill Clinton promised to "end welfare as we know it"
by placing work requirements and time limits on public assis-
tance, among other changes that tacitly drew on the popular economic conception of human decision making and the market
polis. Republicans and Democrats, Tories and New Labour (and
parties throughout the wealthy, global democracies) increasingly

converged in a project of building market poleis for the twenty-first century. In these heady decades, distinctions between the Left and Right began to blur around public claims to neutral, economic science.

Yet as the twenty-first century wore on, there was also a far more radical and drastically unforeseen consequence to reimagining society as a loose network of egoistic dealmakers. Gradually some commentators began arguing that from the perspective of decision science, there was no sharp distinction between vastly different regime types like democracy and dictatorship. This was because all forms of government were organized by the same basic behavioral logic. Democracies and dictatorships both consisted of individuals simply strategizing to maintain as much power as they could for the longest duration of time. After all, the logical conclusion of Mayhew's congressional theory was that career even trumped the norms, term limits, and rules of fair play in a democratic republic.

In any case, this was the portentous argument advanced by two prominent political scientists in 2011. Bruce Bueno de Mesquita and Alastair Smith argued ominously at this time that, viewed through the assumptions of rational choice theory, there were no fundamental ethical or political motives differentiating the leadership in democracies from those in dictatorships. Instead, "any leader worth her salt wants as much power as she can get, and to keep it for as long as possible," and "every type of politics could be addressed from the point of view of leaders trying to survive."[17] This meant "governments do not differ in kind," only in the strategic scenarios they face for holding onto power.[18] Every human leader in the ambit of power was a proto-dictator, and political science was a *Dictator's Handbook*, as the title to their book put it.

Such lines of thinking implied that the moral differences traditionally distinguishing democracies and dictatorships were scientifically irrelevant. This is what the scientific "logic of politics" taught: that this is a "world of self-interested thinking."[19] Moreover, a market polis could be run by either a single ruler or many representatives. The logic of single-person dictatorship was not in its fundamental workings all that different from a legislature. The line between dictatorship and democracy was fuzzy and porous. In short, the distinction between the two opposing regime types had been fully relativized by social "science."

Like economists and the 2008 crash, political scientists such as Bueno de Mesquita and Smith were completely unable to predict one of the largest political events of their lifetimes despite supposedly understanding the basic science of human behavior. Brexit, the election of Trump, and the global ascent of authoritarian and backsliding democracies were not predicted by any major political scientist. Nonetheless, Bueno de Mesquita and Smith did help imagine a world in which nothing was particularly at stake in the passage from democracy to dictatorship. After all, decision science showed that a dictatorial executive was really no different in inner motivations than a democratic legislator. Political scientists like Bueno de Mesquita and Smith had blurred a line in social science that in a few short years would be blurred in the ideological contests of the world.

But in these early years of the millennium, there appeared to be no crisis on the horizon for the various sciences of the market polis. Instead, scientifically guided policy faced no problem too large to resolve. Indeed, because rational choice action was the universal, underlying logic of all human behavior, enlightened policy could trust that it had the tools necessary for curing ills both large and small.

So, for example, from the perspective of this popular science of economics the growing ecological crisis was surmountable by simply building more markets (e.g., carbon credits). In addition, private individuals were responsible for global climate change, not any kind of social or political community as a whole. This meant the rational response could be reduced to minor consumer choices on the margins (e.g., recycling a glass bottle, xeriscaping, buying an electric car, composting). What was certainly off the table were collective movements and forms of association that broke out of the individualistic, market polis mode.

But what if there were a popular swell of support for collective action and government regulation (as there had been a generation earlier in the case of the creation of the Environmental Protection Agency)? This question highlights the way the economic sciences of the market polis are potentially in tension with majority rule. A market polis might require a technocracy: rule by social science and economics experts who could teach, correct, or even outright override wayward democratic majorities.

Free-market economics was not therefore necessarily antistatist or antibureaucratic. Instead, state power was legitimate insofar as it was redesigned according to the dictates of rational choice economics. From this perspective even a dictator who implemented the findings of economic science was in some ways preferable to a legislature that did not. What mattered was that the science of human behavior ruled society.

The result of this massive double-H effect was that the market polis and its constellation of meanings came to be imagined by many people as inescapable. Rival significations of democracy and freedom were either eclipsed or forgotten as prescientific. The political culture of the New Deal and its vision of society as built around solidarity with laborers and their need for economic welfare was rejected. In this context, Franklin Delano Roosevelt's 1936 campaign speech claiming that "the sole thought" of the true representative is "the welfare of the United States of America" made little sense other than as a careerist attempt to claim credit and win a strategic bid for power.

In this way, the theory of rational choice served as a kind of meaning converter, taking older meanings and pushing them through its abstract mechanism, turning them into the meanings of the market polis. Choosing the public good or welfare was simply one person's uppermost preference. What appeared to be an act of neutrally inputting beliefs and meanings into a formal structure of choice in fact substantively changed the nature and content of those beliefs and meanings. Altruism became yet another form of self-interest, public service another kind of careerism.

So triumphant was this economic logic that even the most famous defenders of social democracy in the 1970s reproduced it. For example, many intellectuals on the American Left flocked around the political philosophy of John Rawls, who imagined completely autonomous, rational-choice individuals selecting a society like so many options on a hypothetical menu. Rawls's original position could be read as a soft version of *Homo economicus*, exercising a kind of cautious self-interest about his or her hypothetical prospects in a just society.[20] Political philosophy itself took on the basic concepts of economic and decision science.

Older claims for public spiritedness, patriotism, and civic self-sacrifice sounded naïve and unscientific in the spaces of the market polis. This was in stark contrast to the political culture of early America, which had drawn from the ancient republican tradition and held that the pursuit of private self-interest at the expense of the public good was the key distinguishing feature of unjust, morally corrupt societies. For this reason the American Founders, although they believed self-interest had a role in politics, also insisted on the centrality of patriotic sentiments and virtues.[21] A classic figure of this ethic in the early republic was George Washington, who was reluctant to run for president and once elected refused a third term. Even James Madison, who believed that interest would check interest in a federal society, never imagined that self-interest alone could sustain a republic. As he noted in his speech at the Virginia Ratifying Convention, delivered in June 1788: "Is there no virtue among us? If there be not, we are in a wretched situation. No theoretical checks—no form of government can render us secure. To suppose that any form of government will secure liberty or happiness without any virtue is a chimerical idea."

Within the extremist logic of the market polis, Washington's and Madison's sentiments could not but appear as an alien language from a bygone world. But advocates of the market polis erased this difference by running history itself through the meaning converter of economic logic, rendering the Revolution of 1776 the prequel to the Tea Party of 2009. Economic science created and discovered new pasts suddenly populated by its own postulates. Buchanan had presaged this transformation decades earlier, claiming that applying the economic logic of choice to American public life was not "some profoundly new insight" but rather "incorporates a presupposition about human nature that differs little, if at all, from that which informed the thinking of

James Madison at the American founding" and the "scientific wisdom of the 18th century."[22] In this way, the American republic appeared as if it had always been the republic of rational choice.

Unfortunately for rational-choice economics, the claim to a bona fide science is mired in a number of insoluble problems. As is widely known in academia, psychologists have established that individuals simply do not consistently act according to the maxims of rational choice theory, so the picture is factually false.[23] But the interpretive approach also highlights an even deeper set of problems. Human agency is far more plastic and heterogeneous than rational choice allows. Rational choice fails to explain human behavior because it does not grapple with the range of possible meanings that motivate human life. In the rush to establish a universal, scientific anthropology, this theory neglects human beings' distinguishing feature: their ability to embody meanings.

Human beliefs do not have to take on a particular formal structure. They need not always be transitive, complete, or calculative, or form a kind of hierarchy of preferences. Indeed, humans can even actively cultivate "irrational" ways of acting simply because they wish to be eccentric, perceived as unconventional, or frustrate free-market economists (as W. H. Auden ironically advised: "Thou shalt not . . . commit a social science"). Interpretive theory therefore insists on the profoundly historical and cultural nature of human agency.

The latter also implies that humans can learn to think economically, and interpretive theory would expect to see those who have studied economics extensively (and even those exposed to looser forms of the cultural phenomenon *Homo economicus*) behaving and thinking more consistently "economically" than other agents. This is the result of a double-H effect that allows humans to embody different matrices of meaning and work to approximate their own theories. Thus, when treated as a universal anthropology, rational choice theory actually creates the possibility of deceptive self-confirming, looping effects.

Popular, vulgarized forms of high economic theory can be lived out as ethical-ideological options. This complicates the common view that economic science is a completely value-neutral, ideology-free endeavor. For instance, Milton Friedman's famous claim that economics was a "positive" and "objective science" that was "independent of any particular ethical position" is misleading at best.[24] At least in the case of the ideal of human agency assumed by many economic theories, there are deep ethical and ideological potentialities. What appears to be an act of highly technical description is also at one and the same time an act of meaning creation and moral and political imagination. Indeed, all of modern social science may be read as a kind of repressed imaginative literature in which new identities are continually dreamt up.

One never simply discovers the fact that humans are fundamentally economic agents, in the way that natural scientists discover that genes have a particular nucleic acid sequence. Rather, the very discovery of economic man was part of the creation of economic man. Perhaps it would be best to say that free-market economists did not unearth the world but helped to contrive it.

PART II

I, Robot

Genes and Machines

Something strange happened in science fiction dramas in the 2000s: the robots, increasingly played by actors, were depicted as more human than the humans. Two of the most popular examples of this, *Westworld* and *Ex Machina*, both obsessively played on the visual trick that the robots onscreen might later turn out to be humans and vice versa. In doing so they rejected the obvious mechanical androids of earlier sci-fi films, like *Star Wars*'s C-3PO and R2-D2. Instead, in the opening of *Westworld* a male character asked his female host, "Are you real?" She replied, "Well, if you can't tell, does it matter?"

Such anxieties about machine turned man were not new to the history of film and dated back to Fritz Lang's brilliant 1920s classic *Metropolis*. But in *Metropolis* the entrancing Maschinenmensch played by Brigitte Helm was an unambiguously evil foil to her human counterpart. By contrast, *Westworld* and *Ex Machina* implied that robots might surpass humans in their very humanity. In other words, there might be no bright line dividing the humans from the machines anymore. Viewers of these films were being taught to imagine themselves as existing on a spectrum of robots.

No less strange is that *Westworld* and *Ex Machina* both popularized an academic theory of intelligence known as the Turing test. The famous mathematician Alan Turing had invented this test many decades earlier. Turing believed that a machine would count as artificially intelligent (i.e., as "AI") when it could deceive humans into believing it was a fellow human being in a blind conversation. *Ex Machina* went so far as to explicitly explain the Turing test to viewers before launching into a series of plot twists in which the audience's ability to distinguish the AIs from the humans was increasingly confounded. The film climaxed in a bloodbath in which human characters were left for dead in the wilderness while AIs self-emancipated and entered civilization. As the fictional inventor of AI, a mad genius named Nathan, foretold in the movie's key dialogue: "One day the AIs are going to look back on us the same way we look at fossil skeletons . . . an upright ape living in dust with crude language and tools, all set for extinction."

The popularity of *Ex Machina* and *Westworld* coincides with a heated debate over the role of AI and computing machines in modern societies. The United States in particular is immersed in deep anxieties about mechanization, the effects of computer technologies on social life, the gig economy, and the loss of traditional forms of work to robotics. On one side of the debate are tech doomsayers, typified by business tycoon Elon Musk. Following the Swedish philosopher Nick Bostrom, Musk has warned his followers that AI robots are on the verge of making a great leap forward that will mark them off as an independent line of evolution, and that they will usurp human dominance of the globe. If we are not careful, *Homo sapiens* will be relegated to inferior species status (AI's "house cats," as Musk put it).

On the other side are tech boosters like Mark Zuckerberg, who publicly denounce Musk's "doomsday scenario" as "irresponsible." Zuckerberg is a longtime promoter of Silicon Valley technologies and their ability to improve human life. For Zuckerberg technologies like his own Facebook and AI are the positive result of human innovation. Zuckerberg and his followers believe AI will increase productivity, improve services, facilitate new job creation, and promote human flourishing. AI and a computerized economy are to be embraced.

From the perspective of interpretive philosophy, however, what makes this debate notable are not the differences between doomsayers and boosters but their unspoken, deep agreement. Specifically, both sides accept the basic premise that computational systems are capable of attaining and even superseding human intelligence. They achieve this tacit consensus, moreover, because of a shared faith in a metaphor crafted by researchers in the social sciences. This is the anthropological metaphor of *Homo machina*, or humans conceived as highly complex machines. Of course the metaphor (like all metaphors) has recognized limits: for instance, engineers intentionally design and create machines, while nature accidentally produces humans out of a process of random molecule mutation. But although not designed, according to this vision the human species is nonetheless a system of mechanics akin to engineered androids.

This anthropological metaphor has deep roots in the history of the social sciences. In fact, the idea that humans might be conceptualized as natural or "wet" machines is nearly as old as the scientific revolution itself and was born with the nascent social sciences. In the early 1600s, Galileo had already formulated the notion of a machine as a system of mechanical parts operated by input energy. At nearly the same time, philosophers who contributed to the founding of the modern social sciences, such as Thomas Hobbes, offered speculative machinist accounts of human nature, as in the opening pages of his masterwork *Leviathan*, in which he asked: "Why may we not say that all *Automata* (Engines that move themselves by springs and wheels as doth a watch) have an artificial life? For what is the *Heart* but a *Spring*, and the *Nerves*, but so many *Strings*; and the *Joints* but so many *Wheels*, giving motion to the whole Body?"[1]

A century later the French philosopher Julien Offray de La Mettrie repeated the machine metaphor in even blunter form in his influential tract, *Man a Machine*. La Mettrie had become convinced that all higher order human capacities were determined by the mechanics of muscles. Indeed, according to La Mettrie, "the human body is a watch" that "winds its own springs," and "the brain has its muscles for thinking, as the legs have muscles for walking."[2] In this way, Hobbes and Le Mettrie helped inaugurate a speculative tradition in the human sciences in which the latest developments of technology are used to reverse engineer the workings of human behavior.

More sophisticated theorizations of the machine metaphor were devised in the twentieth century. For example, the American psychologist B. F. Skinner led a widely influential research program known as behaviorism, which taught that human beings were a kind of stimulus-response contraption, continually shaped and triggered by the environment around them.[3] More recently machinist anthropologists turned to neuroscience and the structures of the brain. Social scientists inspired by these discoveries even attempted to construct a total neuroscience of human behavior, inventing fields such as neuroeconomics, neuropolitics, neuroethics, and neurolaw. Defenders of these re-search programs believed all the social sciences would eventually become immersed in "the advancing tide of neuroscience."[4]

But perhaps the most popular account of *Homo machina* to date (and certainly the model that forms the background of pop-ular culture phenomena like *Ex Machina* and *Westworld*) was born out of a synthesis of cognitive psychology and computer sci-ence. Just as Hobbes and La Mettrie noticed that the state of art in technology was the mechanics of a watch and imagined humans accordingly, cognitive scientists working in the late twentieth cen-tury recognized that the state of art in technology was computers and conceptualized a computational view of humans. Harvard cognitive psychologist Steven Pinker is the most formidable pop-ularizer of this anthropological metaphor, conferring upon it a broad cultural authority. In his 1997 book *How the Mind Works*, Pinker laid out the basic outlines of what cognitive psychologists called the "computational theory of mind."

According to Pinker, the computer revolution allowed psychologists to envision how mind, consciousness, and in-telligence might be a feature of a system composed of "life-less gumball-machine parts."[5] The key breakthrough was Alan Turing's envisioning of a symbol-processing machine. Turing was the first to picture a machine that would combine the automatic triggers of traditional mechanics with the symbolic relationships of an algorithm. Such "Turing machines" could in principle ex-ecute a simple fixed set of steps like a recipe by initiating a basic series of causal mechanisms. As Pinker put it, the computational revolution was inspired by the insight that symbolic calculations could be carried out by "arrangements of matter" that had "both representational and causal properties . . . that simultaneously carry information about something and take part in a chain of physical events."[6]

In cognitive psychology this meant that a crucial step in understanding the human mind was mapping the basic conceptual features of computer technology in order to reverse engineer (at least in abstract theoretical terms) a human brain. Much of Pinker's account of the mechanics of the human brain was an effort to speculatively imagine this organ of soft nerve tissue as a form of symbol processor. At the center of this metaphor was the view that the brain was the "hardware" of chemical processes, while the mind was the "software" of algorithmic steps or informational processing. Indeed, for Pinker the metaphor of a computer clarified the basic disciplinary boundaries for scientifically studying human beings. Neurobiology would focus on investigating the biological "hardware," while psychology would inquire into the "mental software."[7]

Pinker declared that with the brain as a neurobiological computer and the mind as its software, ordinary people could grasp the basic metaphors of a universal science of human behavior. The self, society, language, morality, politics and the arts would all be decoded as evolutionary software, determined by neurological hardware. Ultimately cognitive neuroscience would show that "every aspect of our mental lives depends entirely on physiological events in the tissues of the brain."[8] The notion that human mind and intelligence were essentially algorithmic persisted in later popularizations of computational theory promoted by those computer scientists like Andrew Ng who taught massive online seminars on the engineering behind "neural networks" that allowed machines to execute tasks they were not explicitly programmed to achieve beforehand. This used the technology of machine learning (the basis for self-driving cars, photo and voice recognition, and other cutting-edge computer applications) to imply that human intelligence operated essentially in the same manner.

What is of primary importance from this discussion is not initially whether the computational theory of mind or the other social scientific theories backing *Homo machina* are correct or true to reality. Rather, the point for my analysis is the way that these theories are always at the same time a form of meaning creation: a suggestive, imaginative act that enters the popular realm and shapes the ethical and political practices of contemporary society. In other words, my focus in what follows is to argue via examples that the extended highly complex metaphor of *Homo machina* (like all social science) does not solely exist on the page, as it were, but becomes flesh and creates a world. This repressed feature of the social scientific theories extending from Hobbes to Pinker is a blind spot in their own theorization. What claims to be merely an act of discovery is in fact always also an act of ethical and ideological creation. But to say this is already to point beyond the metaphor of man as simply a computational mechanics.

MELANCHOLY MACHINES

Outside of high academe, how was the metaphor of humans as neurobiological computational machines lived in actual, vulgarized practice? One of the most common ways that neurobiological accounts of *Homo machina* entered the cultural world was via various therapeutic and clinical practices for modulating human mood and behavior. In clinical settings individuals had long learned to interpret themselves through the metaphor of a complex neurobiological machine. Specifically, depression, anxiety, and other maladies were said to stem from chemical imbalances in the brain. As Pinker put it, depressed people's "brains . . . are not working properly" and "tweaking the brain with drugs may sometimes be the best way to jump-start the machinery that we call the will."[9]

A reader of Pinker's writings was thus already well on the way to imagining himself or herself as a machine in need of brute physical interventions to treat conditions like depression. No longer was depression or anxiety a mood that attuned an individual to the reality of loss or injustice within society. Rather than having existential, spiritual, or political meaning, the significance of depression was reduced to a mechanics by the metaphor of *Homo machina*. There were clear religious and political implications to interpreting experiences of depression and anxiety in this way.

The biochemical model for depression gained truly astonishing momentum during the twentieth century as psychologists worked in tandem with a growing mass-market pharmaceutical industry. A common culprit for depression and anxiety was said to be the genetic machinery for serotonin uptake in the brain. Low serotonin levels were correlated with a diminishment in what psychologists termed "prosocial" behaviors: actions that helped promote social connectedness. Potential patients—both current and future sufferers of depression—were educated into an entire system of symbols and meanings. Depression as a set of feelings was epiphenomenal to "cocktails" of chemicals washing over the brain. The key to wellness was to readjust these chemical washes into the right admixture. Depression was not a wrestling with existential or political meanings but closer to repairing a highly complex car, and as with automotive mechanics, one must entrust one's money and well-being to the experts.

From the beginning this ethical-scientific practice was justified in terms of therapeutic results. That is, the successful outcomes of treating oneself *as if* one were a chemical machine were offered as crucial evidence for the truth of the biochemical theory of depression itself. As Alec Coppen, an early pioneer in this area of psychopharmacology, put it: "One of the most cogent reasons for believing that there is a biochemical basis for depression . . . is the astonishing success of physical methods of treatment of these conditions."[10] Thus this version of *Homo machina*—in which patients treated themselves like biochemical machines in need of pharmacological intervention—was not a set of abstract beliefs or doctrines but a set of lived practices. The theories helped patients imagine themselves according to a mechanical metaphor, and the practice of treating oneself in this way was offered as verification of the truth of the science. The metaphor was therefore lived as an integral part of its justification as a hypothesis. This constitutes nothing short of a dramatically explicit case of a looping double-H effect (in which interpretations of social reality penetrate and radically change that social reality).

Of course this set of practices en masse presupposed the modern pharmaceutical industry. This was not only for the material and chemical capacities necessary to manufacture millions of pills; the pharmaceutical industry was also instrumental in advertising and selling the metaphors and meanings of *Homo machina* to ordinary citizens. Advertisements for antidepressants often presented dosage charts linked to photographs of individuals enjoying recovered well-being after being "overwhelmed by sadness" or "feeling down."[11] Consumerism thus took on a pedagogical function, exhorting and persuading ordinary citizens to treat themselves as if they were neurochemical hardware. Such lessons were lent scientific authority by cadres of experts educated in psychology departments and armed with the latest machinist theories of the mind.

Demand for such a therapeutic was also generated through aggressive advertising. In the mid-twentieth-century the American government heavily regulated this kind of advertising, and major pharmaceutical companies were only allowed to peddle their products to medical doctors, who held the power of prescription. But beginning in the 1980s and 1990s, under the heavy influence of the free-market science of economics and its model of the inherently rational consumer (apparently even those dealing with potentially debilitating mental illness), government officials deregulated this aspect of the pharmaceutical economy and allowed corporations to advertise everything from antidepressants to opioid painkillers directly to average Americans. Such direct-to-consumer advertising presented more simplified accounts of depression than those offered in the specialized genre of the technical discourses of psychiatric and psychological science. Indeed, studies of the commercial culture surrounding the sale of antidepressants like Prozac found that antidepressant advertising consistently "propagate[d] narrowly biological explanations of depression."[12]

Critics of the science behind this therapeutic mined statistical evidence demonstrating that antidepressant pills and their effectiveness were largely the result of a placebo effect. The psychologist Irving Kirsch authored a widely debated empirical study that found "most of the improvement shown by depressed people when they take antidepressants is due to the placebo effect."[13]

This suggested that the entire social ritual of advertising, submission to scientific authority, and taking pills was itself the major ingredient in treating anxiety and depression. The meanings and practices were the stuff of the therapeutic and not any particular active chemical in the medicines. Indeed, the studies suggested that the chemicals themselves were no more the causal mechanism behind curing depression than would be the sugar in a dummy pill. As in earlier forms of magic from a prescientific age, ritualistic performance of the theory was essential to its causal effects, except that these rituals were said to be carried out in the name of "science," and in place of magicians one had the person of the biochemical clinician. Scientific authority morphing into scientism had thus conjured forth the return of ritualized magic.

In short, what antidepressant pharmacology offered was not foremost a scientific theory but an ethical-political practice, a method that used the language and authority of science to offer a discipline for the transformation of self. This self viewed the sources of the malaise as entirely materialistic, barring any serious standing for spiritual or political grievances. The material practice had therefore gained a kind of status as a very peculiar modern form of consumer ascesis.

Indeed, one of the most widely read popular books advocating the use of antidepressants made this very point. Psychiatrist Peter Kramer, in his massively popular *Listening to Prozac*, suggested that antidepressants might be used not merely to treat depression but also to generate certain types of personalities that were deemed socially attractive: energetic, confident, sociable, and highly productive in the workplace. For Kramer the main significance of an antidepressant like Prozac was its ability to generate a type of fundamental conversion. "My concern," Kramer wrote, drawing on his own experiences as a clinician, "has been . . . people who are not so much cured of illness as transformed."[14] Indeed, Kramer believed he stood at the threshold of an epoch-making discovery in psychology, from which a new kind of modern self would emerge. The point was not whether antidepressants like Prozac were good or bad but that "it is impossible to imagine the modern world without them."[15] A new Prozac-induced self was emerging within the field of history.

Although not unaware of the ethical and political complexities of his thesis, Kramer primarily saw himself not as exhorting the creation of the Prozac-self but as describing a fait accompli. Antidepressants were already being combined with the scientific authority of researchers and clinicians in an effort to produce Prozac-molded identities. In this respect, critics of the ethical dimensions of antidepressants were engaging the issue at a much deeper level than those who simply observed the manifest empirical flaws of the chemical-imbalance theory of depression. For example, Gary Greenberg argued that uniformly treating depression and anxiety as diseases contributed to an ideological agenda in which a sense of malaise or discontent with a reigning social-political order was stigmatized.[16] The result of such psychopharmacology was to generate compliant, industrious, and dutiful members of society. Greenberg thus in some senses accepted Kramer's analysis but turned the ethical significance on its head: the problem with antidepressants was primarily ethical and only secondarily scientific. Similarly, studies like those by Oliver James in Britain suggested that levels of depression, anxiety, and other maladies were social in origin, appearing at much higher rates in hyper-individualistic, materialistic societies than in other political orders.[17] The practice of reducing depression to material causes therefore served the ideological function of shielding a society of mass consumerism from its share of the responsibility for the crisis.

Thus, while the popularized sciences of depression may not cure these maladies on their own terms, they do participate in a constellation of hyper-individualistic, materialist practices that help shape and manage them. In cases such as attention deficit/hyperactivity disorder (ADHD), the more people interpret themselves through these scientific categories, the higher the incidence of the disease. Gregg Henriques has noted that the scientists who first developed the categories of ADHD hypothesized that only 1 to 2 percent of children would exhibit such a pathology, but by 2013 nearly 15 percent of American high schoolers had been diagnosed with the disease and treated with pharmaceuticals.[18]

This unintended consequence of the theory suggests that in addition to an official empirical theory, also generated at the popular political level was a set of meanings that was enacted into the practices of a modern ascesis. Where once students and their parents might have interpreted energy and concentration problems under a different cultural rubric (e.g., as a sign that there was a need to reform traditional schooling *or* as an area for developing Aristotle's notion of moral excellence or *arête*), now the phenomenon of restlessness in a classroom was pathologized and perceived as disease by the students themselves. Moreover, the problem was rooted in brain programming, largely outside of individual volition. Students saw and experienced themselves through the robotic metaphor of *Homo machina*. Thus, the first-person experience of fidgeting and having difficulty concentrating was altered by the entry of the scientific category. With the new science came new meanings, significances, and ethical coordinates. A double-H effect had led to an epidemic of distraction and restlessness. Social science inadvertently created, where it had only meant to discover, a new world.

RED STATE, BLUE STATE ROBOTS

A less well-known way in which neuroscientific visions of *Homo machina* infiltrated and helped shape the cultural world was via political science. For several generations American political scientists had been warning the general public about extreme party polarization. Not only did adherents of the two major parties oppose each other in politics, but increasingly they lived in different communities, married different people, ate different foods, worshipped in different places, and isolated themselves in different cultures. A "Red" Republican America versus a "Blue" Democratic America was emerging, with the red areas becoming redder and the blue ones bluer. Many wondered how much longer a society of such intense animosities could hold together before flying apart.

Amid these ongoing developments in the early 2000s three researchers—John Alford, Carolyn Funk, and John Hibbing—argued that political attitudes reflected deep genetic programming in the biological hardware of individuals. Drawing from twin studies, they hypothesized that genes working in conjunction with environmental factors determined political attitudes, especially ideological commitments, in ways of which "the actors themselves are not consciously aware."[19]

This entire approach to political explanation eventually became known as "genopolitics." According to Alford, Funk, and

Hibbing, political ideologies like liberalism and conservatism, while not entirely determined by structures in the brain, were nevertheless largely inherited biological traits. The offspring of conservative parents tended to be conservative, and the offspring of liberal parents, liberal—but this was not due to the socialization process or education but rather hardwired tendencies deep within the genetic code. This was also said to help explain the "consistency in ideological divisions that [was] present across space and time" and the "package of attitudes" that divided "virtually all polities, and certainly the United States in the early twenty-first century."[20]

Specifically, these researchers argued that conservatives gathered around absolutism, dogmatism, and hierarchy, while liberals gravitated toward openness, tolerance, and egalitarianism. Of course such biological explanations of liberal versus conservative erased the fact that historians of political thought had long before shown these ideological traditions were highly variant, far from timeless, and emerged in particular cultural contexts. In addition, the portrait of the two ideologies appeared tacitly biased. How many American conservatives, for example, would accept the labels dogmatic and absolutist as core features of their political positions?

The authors seemed to create natural, necessary bonds out of features that could easily vary across individuals; for example, one could be an absolutist liberal with a preference for hierarchy (like the American economist James Buchanan) or a conservative who preferred openness and tolerance (like the British political philosopher Michael Oakeshott). Liberal and conservative, in other words, were not being treated as interpretive meanings that could be creatively modified but as fundamental, unchangeable objects.

In this way, genopolitics turned "Blue" liberals and "Red" conservatives into naturally occurring personality types and even distinct psychological tribes of people. A reader of genopolitics would learn that in some senses the liberal-conservative split was simply written into human DNA. This offered a mode of self-interpretation and a set of social coordinates that readers could then enact in their own lives. Indeed, since the authors believed that individuals preferred to pair with like-minded mates, the intensity of genetic polarization was only strengthened through breeding practices. Those learning about genopolitics should expect not to be attracted to members of the other party. This was not a moral limitation or failure of wider human solidarity but simply biology. One's own spiritual and political biases and failings had been laundered into mere facts of biological "science."

The hypotheses of these political scientists and other proponents of genopolitics reached a wider audience through journalists such as Chris Mooney and his 2012 book *The Republican Brain: The Science of Why They Don't Believe in Science*, as well as the writings of *New York Times* columnist Thomas Edsall. In this way, the ahistorical conception of political attitudes articulated by genopolitics was disseminated into the wider political world, offering Americans scientific categories for interpreting their own perplexing sense of extreme and growing polarization. Suddenly the readers of popular works on genopolitics had a justification for their own mounting discord.

No longer were such beliefs the product of rational conviction and discussion. Rather, they were pre-rational, biological brain settings. Being rationally persuaded by the other side was a fool's errand. Was there any remedy to such tribally hardwired preconfigurations? Could two such hardwired biological tribes even share a consensual, democratic society? One solution to this conundrum weighed by Alford, Funk, and Hibbing was genetically mating the two sides to help moderate political polarization. Unfortunately, reducing the divide in this way was not viable because these researchers believed mate choice tended toward those with similar attitudes. (Quietly, in the margins of the text, the reader can't help imagining a possible society with forced marriage rituals between Democrats and Republicans, just as European monarchs intermarried between dynasties in an effort to balance political power.)

More immediately, the discourse of genopolitics opened the possibility of a feedback loop between the social scientific metaphor of machine programming and a hardening of political outlooks within the culture. Readers of genopolitical literature were invited to consider themselves and their political attitudes as unchangeable, hardwired, and robotic. Their mushrooming dislike for the opposite side stemmed from their own inner, cold, machine-like nature. One could intensify one's political hatreds all on the basis of a scientific authority that had uncovered these identities encoded into the natural genetic hardware. Indeed, one was not intensifying anything but merely discovering the hard facts that were already there.

This in turn had the potential to lead to a deeper sense of cultural despair over a widening political chasm. While Alford, Funk, and Hibbing suggested their research might be a first step to understanding across political divides, the very reverse was happening in the culture. The metaphor of conservative versus liberal brains was potentially being incorporated into human self-understanding and encouraging prejudicial behavior against the other side. Perhaps liberals and conservatives had already experienced difficulty in forming friendships, let alone marriages. But now they learned that science showed the idea of amity between them was far-fetched. Science had weighed in on the likelihood of affection. Research claiming merely to explain party polarization could enter the loop of meanings and help exacerbate it. The social scientific explanation—supposedly a description standing outside of social relations—had imperceptibly become a part of what still remained in need of explaining: Why were we so divided?

The entire foregoing analysis of double-H effects implies that there is something remarkable about humans that drastically differs from machines and makes the metaphor of *Homo machina* misleading at best. Even the most sophisticated machines engineered to date lack an experience of meaning or purpose as integral to their actions. The philosopher John Searle famously argued that the major distinction between even the most sophisticated computers and human beings was this "semantic" feature. Where a computer processed a formal algorithm (what Searle called "syntax"), humans experienced states of meaning that were the very stuff of consciousness.[21] In fact, computers had long been able to outperform the human mind in running algorithmic calculations. But for the computer there was no inherent meaning or semantic content to this process. In other words, the central feature of specifically human intelligence was missing: that things *matter* to a human being.

By contrast, things do not matter to a computing machine, nor does a symbol processor experience meanings that orient it toward a purpose or goal. A computing (or any other kind of) machine does not experience disappointment, shame, triumph, fellow feeling, or pride when executing its operations. And faster and faster algorithms do nothing to narrow this yawning gap between semantics and syntax. This is because although computer engineers have accomplished vastly impressive feats, they have yet to bring machines a single step closer to the experience of meaning that makes the double-H effect possible in the first place. As the interpretive philosopher Charles Taylor put it, machines are missing a "significance feature," which is crucial to all purposive agents, such that when it comes to the question "what is [that machine] really doing? There is no answer . . . attributions of action-terms to such devices are relative to our interests and purposes."[22]

In other words, when it comes to bridging the gap between syntax and semantics, computers are no closer than the most rudimentary tools from the distant past. After all, the light from a computer screen might be used as an impromptu lantern in a dark room even as the device runs algorithms designed to flash certain symbols on the screen. The computer's process has no more intrinsic meaning than a hammer or any other human tool, which as an instrument can be made to serve different ends.

This suggests that the metaphor of *Homo machina* has the whole relationship between humans and machines backward. We are not computational machines, but in a culture of scientism we poeticize to trick ourselves into making our computing machines appear more like us. Like ancient pagans who found the agency of gods and spirits in rivers and earthquakes, we humanize or anthropomorphize our machines. Again, scientific authority is paradoxically involved in what is often taken to be a centrally prescientific way of thinking. This anthropomorphizing of machinery is a spellbinding act that we experience as if it were a metaphysical reality. Overawed by our own imaginative powers and meaning-making abilities, we see in technology something that is not there: human purposive intelligence. There is indeed an entire metaphorical poetics behind this anthropomorphizing move. Thus we frequently say that the computer is "calculating," "working," "learning," and "thinking" when it is in fact, strictly speaking, doing no such thing.

Does this mean AI is impossible? Not necessarily; it simply shifts the goal of genuine AI from symbol processing to a form of agency capable of purposive experiences of meaning. Everything else is highly sophisticated tool making and nothing more. But a future Alan Turing might yet imagine how the gap between syntax and semantics can be bridged. In any case, the refutation of the computational theory of mind is not my main point here. My point is to suggest that the significance feature of human intelligence is what makes much of the social sciences a poeticizing, creative act of meaning and not merely a descriptive science of the world that was already there waiting for us. The condition for the possibility of the double-H effects discussed here is a being who experiences meanings; this is the stuff of human agency, not algorithmic calculation, which is something that even the greatest savants among us do only mediocrely.

In this regard, a far better proposal for evaluating AI than the Turing test is suggested by the science fiction classic *Blade Runner*. This film—based on a novel by Philip K. Dick—opens with a scene depicting an interview in which a human is testing for the presence of AI. The test requires determining whether an android (known in the movie as a "replicant") is capable of empathy. Empathy is a state that involves an awareness of how another person is experiencing a situation: what matters to him or her and what the emotional significance of a set of circumstances might be. This is closer to the criterion for human intelligence that Searle calls "semantics" and Taylor the "significance" factor. A reworked Turing test would need to be able to determine if an agent were experiencing significance or meanings. Such a test would be an interpretive or hermeneutic threshold for intelligence.

Blade Runner also serves as a powerful interpretive fable for the anxieties surrounding technological society. Taking place in a future version of Los Angeles, the plot follows a man named Deckard, whose profession is "blade running," or hunting and destroying rogue replicants. Yet Deckard finds himself increasingly disturbed and alienated not only by his own severe loss of empathy for those around him but also by the atomized social relations of an impersonal, consumer society dominated by distant corporations. In this setting an awakening of empathy comes from a strange place: Deckard falls in love with one of the replicants he has been hired to kill.

At the center of this story is a deeper cultural fear that is the actual, repressed object of anxiety in the contemporary AI debate between doomsayers and boosters. This is a repressed fear of ourselves and what we might become if we go further down the road of the form of selfhood presented by *Homo machina*. That is to say, fear of robots is fear of ourselves without humanity, without empathy. Or perhaps more accurately, fear of AI is fear not of technology but of a new constellation of meanings opened up by technological society. The machine-self is one possible form of identity that humans embody in a culture of scientism.

This in turn might be linked to the distinctively modern cultures of violence—as scientifically planned by military experts and technocrats—so common in societies across the ideological spectrum. Consider in this light Joseph Stalin's conviction that social science had revealed society could be explained "in accordance with the laws of movement of matter."[23] This machine view of society was the prologue to treating people like basic parts, to be replaced with other purportedly better parts. Stalinism was only one extreme version of the propensity of modern societies to conduct "scientific" mass killings. This is the kind of killing carried out remotely and planned by scientific experts. A dark dream that began in the French Revolution with the guillotine has reached an apotheosis with the invention of the concentration camp-laboratory, where violence is perfectly justified because it is perfectly rational. There is no "I" behind the system of violence in the camp-laboratory; neither is there a "you" on the receiving end. In the last analysis, there is only the impersonal mechanics of a machine grinding humanity into cinder and fire.

In *Blade Runner* we are offered a capitalist version of this mechanistic culture of violence and antihumanism. The humans who populate a future, dystopian Los Angeles have become radically more robotic in this way; they are no longer attuned to the experiences of their neighbors and are willing to treat them like mute objects. The streets of this Los Angeles are filled with a babble of tongues, homeless people dig through the trash, and crowds rush through the sidewalks distracted by their own individual market activity. No one speaks to one another, while neon advertisements shout platitudes about enjoying soft drinks or starting a new life on an "off-world" colony in outer space. Deckard at one point remarks that his ex-wife used to call him a "cold fish," but the audience is relentlessly confronted with an entire society of cold fishes. What distinguishes Deckard is that he struggles mightily throughout the film to overcome his hardened willingness to assassinate others as simply part of his job, a mere market transaction. The entire plot is thus absorbed in the problem of the loss of human empathy and its replacement with a roboticized self that sees all relationships—even those of violence—as mechanical and rational. In all these ways, the city and inhabitants depicted in *Blade Runner* are not a portrait of the future at all but a dramatic picture of the present: the world as built by *Homo machina*.

The Management Ethos

One of the most popular television series in the United States and Britain in the early 2000s was *The Office*, a satire of white-collar desk work. In both the British original and American remake, the same basic story unfolded: an intelligent but frustrated pair of protagonists found themselves inundated by pointless paperwork, boring meetings, and workplace incompetence. Atop the pyramid sat a manager, the person in the office who least contributed to the actual daily work and lacked a valuable skillset. This was in spite of the fact that as manager he was presumably paid the most, a form of inequality justified by the authority of managers as experts in the rational organization of the workplace. And yet *The Office* relentlessly depicted the manager as uniquely irrational and lacking in social intelligence: unable to connect with his subordinates; manipulating others in meetings and management exercises; and addicted to a misguided bonhomie that bottomed out into inadvertent racism, sexism, and buffoonery. In other words, *The Office* was among other things an extended satire on the bogus authority of the management class. Lacking humanistic feeling and intelligence, the manager was depicted as submerged in ineffectual attempts at manipulating those around him into greater "productivity."

Of course humans in all times and places have devised novel and cunning ways to manipulate one another. But *The Office* tapped into the uniquely modern mode of exercising control over each other in the name of management "science." This form of power has entered into the minutia of everyday life, even exercised by ordinary individuals in the privacy of their intimate relationships. In some senses we have all become managers, and the satire applies to every one of us: consumers of a sprawling self-help literature and popular articles in newspapers and magazines that teach us the "sciences" of how to manage love, family life, friendships, finances, personal well-being, happiness, and nearly every other facet of existence. Scientific rationality is said to help us gain control of our circumstances and how others treat us. We struggle to become the effective managers of our own lives.

At the same time, the authority of "science" is also wielded in a more overtly hierarchical manner that excludes many from the decision-making that shapes their lives. This is done through the ascendancy of technocracy or rule by those who claim rational, scientific expertise over the major institutions of society. When technocrats govern in both the public and private spheres, they often install regimes of assessment and copious paperwork that appears to be written in objective and neutral language. Those not conversant with or deemed experts in these managerial idioms (employees and subordinates) are subjected to continual regimes of measurement and training. Indeed, technocrats largely rule by establishing a dominant and official workplace language that marginalizes the meanings, culture, and forms of expression of ordinary people. This approach

derives from the fact that technocrats believe such a specialized language captures the workings of human behavior in a
given institutional setting (everywhere from legislatures and
corporations to universities and schools). Much of what is com-
monly called "management speak" is the language of technocracy, shaped by an eclectic variety of social science concepts,
methods, and theories.

What lurks behind both technocracy and the scientistic self-
help phenomenon is a particular ethical outlook. It might be
called the management ethos, which approaches human life not
primarily as a space of humanistic meanings and narrative history (let alone open, egalitarian dialogue) but as a field of applied science. The management ethos seeks to engineer human
relationships in a manner analogous to how technologists use
the theoretical insights of physics and chemistry to construct
bridges, computers, or telephones. Only the materials in this case
are actual human beings (or "human resources" in the language
of management speak). We presently inhabit a world dominated
by the management ethos, in which humans are reduced to mere
resources for rational control. This chapter examines the management will to power and a culture in which we treat others—
and are in turn treated by others—as scientifically manipulable
human resources.

SEIZING CONTROL OF LOVE AND ALLURE

Many contemporary people seeking to gain control over their
personal lives go in search of scientifically validated techniques.
Beginning from urgent financial, romantic, familial, and even

spiritual problems, the management ethos involves taking a step back from the exigencies of life into a stance of rational detachment. In this view, the way to cope with life's problems is to master a series of techniques and forms of knowledge gleaned from across the natural and social sciences.

One common way to do this is via a popularized, practical form of "scientific method." Though derived from an idealized picture of the method of the natural sciences, this use of method is not the same thing. In popular discourse, the scientific method is often held up as the gold standard differentiating science from all supposedly inferior forms of knowing reality (like the humanities, arts, philosophy, and religion). In broadest terms, a method is a formal set of rules or procedures that if executed successfully guarantees an outcome. For example, in the *Principia Mathematica* Isaac Newton famously formulated four "regulae" or rules of inquiry into the natural world, which were later simplified into popular maxims such as relying only on observation when making scientific hypotheses and treating all findings as revisable in light of future evidence.[1]

Although philosophers generally reject the idea of a single, unified scientific method, the notion has gained a grip on the popular imagination. There is, so to speak, a madness for method in our societies. What method holds out is the promise of forcing people and circumstances into predictable outcomes. In the self-help literature and popular press this is expressed in endless lists of scientifically validated "steps" necessary for achieving a vast variety of life goals. As with the treatment of depression, there is an entire repressed ideology and rigid ethical discipline that assumes the rhetoric of bona fide science. Here I critically dissect two brief examples from mass culture.

The first is drawn from the self-help literature on erotic love and dating. *Algorithms to Live By*, written by Brian Christian and Tom Griffiths (a Princeton professor of cognitive psychology) transfers the way computers and computer scientists solve problems to the domain of human life. Over the course of the book this approach is said to solve an astonishingly wide range of everyday problems, from renting an apartment to seeking a spouse. Christian and Griffiths advise readers to utilize an algorithm they call the "37 percent rule" when on the hunt for a spouse. This rule holds that because individuals have a finite amount of time and resources to attract mates, they ought to optimize their decision by neither concluding their search too early (before seeing enough "data") nor carrying on too long (after losing the best opportunity likely to come along). "Look at the first 37%" of choices, they explain, "choosing none, then be ready to leap for anyone better than all those you've seen so far."[2] The 37 percent rule means that an individual searching for a spouse between "ages eighteen to forty" should mark "26.1 years as the point at which to switch from looking to leaping."[3]

What follows from Christian and Griffiths's algorithmic analysis is clearly a method for dating: for example, refrain from forming too intense an affection for a single person before twenty-six years of age. In this view, the whole notion of a lifelong attachment, emerging out of adolescence or early adulthood and resulting in marriage, is not scientifically or rationally optimal. This is because anyone who forms loyalties of this kind has failed to gather enough empirical input to run the right statistical calculation (though of course a person who stops searching early might always get lucky).

But closer scrutiny reveals that Christian and Griffiths do not offer a neutral or scientific method for action but rather a new set of meanings that subtly usurp and replace other meanings of erotic love. For example, the Romantic tradition—which marks a major rival to the scientistic tradition in our society—holds that love involves the search for a unique person, expressive of one particular point in time. This alternative view of love is captured in Edgar Allan Poe's famous poem about Annabel Lee: "I was a child and she was a child, / In this kingdom by the sea, / But we loved with a love that was more than love / I and my Annabel Lee." In the Romantic view, the meaning or significance of a particular person is not necessarily transferable across other individuals. Annabel Lee is not simply a set of qualities and opportunities to be maximized in comparison to other opportunities. Rather, there is something fundamentally irreplaceable about Annabel Lee—a form of love that Poe depicts as "stronger by far than the love / Of those who were older than we / Of many far wiser than we."

By contrast, the algorithmic approach assumes that erotic love deals not with the event of a single, nontransferable person but with an abstract set of qualities or resources that recur across individuals and can be optimized. In this view a person is not singular and incommensurable in meaning but a composite set of attributes. This is much closer to the economic conception of a commodity as consisting of swappable features and accessories purchased on a market. Where poetry plays an irreplaceable role in the practices of Romantic love (expressing the singularity of the beloved), data analysis and cycling through as many composites as possible within a fixed time becomes the stuff of this "scientific" form of love. A person wishing to grow in the tradition of Romantic love necessarily becomes a reader (and perhaps even writer) of poetry and love letters, while a person in the algorithmic-mode is chiefly concerned with opportunity costs on a marriage market.

Christian and Griffiths seem completely unaware that what they are offering is not a neutral, scientific tool but an ideology of courtship that fits within the predominant shopping practices of consumer capitalism. Once algorithms like the 37 percent rule are placed in a wider cultural context, it becomes possible to see that they are part of a much bigger shift in our society toward virtual, commodified dating spaces (like Tinder and other dating apps) in which one "user" scans massive data banks of other "users" in order to try to identify optimal matches.

In the Romantic tradition of love a term like "user" has a negative connotation, as it implies someone who is willing to instrumentalize the beloved. But in the commodified market spaces of the new courtship, everyone is a "user" whether they recognize it or not (as a fact of decision "science" and revealed preferences, a further dimension of the market polis). One supposed advantage of the algorithmic, user approach is that it is said to offer not only an unsentimental, scientific approach but also much larger data sets and therefore more informed choices. Where the Romantic lover, following Poe, naively leaps too early, the "user" is able to dispassionately deploy the science of decision-making to satisfy certain preferences re-garding a mate. But this control comes at a steep cost. As the preceding line of interpretation makes clear, the meaning of the term "love" has been radically transformed. One who takes the algorithmic approach can never truly love in Poe's sense of the term.

A similarly repressed, hyper-consumerist ideology can be detected throughout much of the self-help genre. Careful interpretation renders this evident in business self-help books such as Olivia Fox Cabane's popular manual on leadership and the "science of personal magnetism," *The Charisma Myth*. Like Christian and Griffiths, Fox Cabane touts credentials from the country's top universities and presents herself as a mere emissary of the latest cognitive and social psychological findings. However, her analysis consists largely of stipulating long lists of fixed rules or methods said to scientifically guarantee the development of personal charisma. Indeed, the central "myth" of charisma is that it is a mystic quality that is inborn and cannot be learned via scientific insight. Readers are taught that anyone can become charismatic as long as they follow a battery of rules, including appearing powerful, being present, emitting warmth, lowering voice intonation at the end of sentences, and pausing for two full seconds before speaking. All these rules, of course, are presented as scientifically validated.

"You'll learn charisma in a methodical, systematic way," Fox Cabane explains to her readers, "the world will become your lab and every time you meet someone, you'll get an opportunity to experiment" until "people go, 'Wow, who's *that*?' "[4] Although Fox Cabane's method is supposed to scientifically guarantee outcomes, equally important is the art of submitting oneself to a rigid ethical discipline that helps one navigate the individualistic spaces of a market society. Fox Cabane's writings and presentations abound in scenarios in which an upwardly mobile meritocrat is on his or her way to an important interview or entering a boardroom for a life-changing presentation. These individualistic, competitive, episodic, and semi-anonymous social settings provide the site for testing one's personal methodological rigor (e.g., "Did I wait for two seconds before speaking, or did I pause awkwardly long?"; "What was I doing with my facial expressions during the interview?").

In its relentlessly disengaged personal moralism and obsessive self-care, the scientistic self-help genre bears a distant echo of the discourses of the ancient Stoics. The locus is no longer the enchanted Stoic cosmos, but the impersonal, ambitious arenas of materialistic commercial society. Indeed, what readers of Fox Cabane's books learn is not so much a scientific theory as an ethos and social script that are said to be scientifically valid. Reading such works is as much about learning how to perform these cultural meanings and what counts as "charismatic" in market societies as it is about uncovering the timeless mechanics of human magnetism. Science is authorizing a form of capitalist culture.

Part of what is missing from Fox Cabane's account is the interpretive insight that charisma (like erotic love) is shaped by cultural meanings and traditions and does not exist in brute, timeless scientific isolation. Fox Cabane's advice that one should appear powerful might plausibly pass for charismatic in competitive market scenarios but not, say, in a religious monastery or artists' commune. Indeed, in many cultural milieus those who follow steps in order to scientifically compel others to be drawn to them qualify as the height of phony and uncharismatic. In other words, these social scientific meanings are much more an enactment, performance, and enforcement of ideology than they are anything having to do with the authority of science.

The circle of the double-H effect is closed as the readers of such books confirm the truth of the theories through their own adoption of the methods into practice. Having read *The Charisma Myth*, readers go forth into the workplace, interviews, conferences, alumni networking events, cocktail parties, and professional mixers ready to perform and see performed this version of charisma. The result is the collective reinforcement of an alarmingly manipulative form of consumer culture, not the official scientific account of things human.

TINKERING WITH DEMOCRACY

This ethos of manipulation, is not only expressed in the voluminous self-help genre but also has entered and helped revamp the discourse surrounding democracy itself. When the term "democracy" was coined in ancient Greece, it meant rule by the *demos* or common people. Later theorists of democracy, such as Alexis de Tocqueville, followed this Greek understanding by arguing that authentic democracy required active, meaningful participation by citizens in ruling and forming laws. However, there is also a long rival tradition of diluting or even changing the meaning of democracy to rule by a group of elites who are said to act in the name of the people. The management ethic has its own way of transforming democracy from rule by the common people to rule by an expert, professional political class.

In the case of this form of technocracy, elites justify their rule based on the purported inability of the common person to think rationally. At the heart of the technocratic conception of "democracy" is the claim that certain elites hold the reins of a predictive science of human behavior unavailable to ordinary people. This can take the form of the technical languages previously described, but it can also be expressed as having discovered impersonal, mechanistic laws governing social life in stable, statistical regularities (e.g., "whenever *A* happens, all things being equal, *B* happens, or is *C* % more likely to happen"). The common person might be morally entitled to choose the ultimate ends of society but must leave determining how to achieve those ends to the real experts, the technocrats.

Such a transformation of the meaning of the word "democracy" is evident in *Nudge*, an influential work of popular social science by Richard Thaler (a Noble-prize-winning economist) and Cass Sunstein (a Harvard law professor). Thaler and Sunstein argue that the basic sociopolitical problem facing society is that individuals regularly succumb to biased thinking and make irrational choices. According to their theory, this is a product of the fact that human thinking is split into two cognitive tiers, one an "automatic" system riddled with biases and irrational intuitions and the other a "reflective and rational" system requiring a high degree of energy and attention to activate.[5]

In normal, everyday life the intuitions of the automatic brain do fairly well, but when faced with complex or unfamiliar choices, they prove disastrous. For instance, Thaler and Sunstein argue that humans are generally highly conformist and tend to follow the herd. This bias is motivated by the intuition that others might hold useful information and therefore their decisions might create a shorthand for the best course of action. But automatically following the herd also leads to many personal and social ills. For instance, college students might turn to binge drinking and citizens might justify not paying taxes, both based on the false perception that everyone else is doing so with good cause.

Much of *Nudge* consists of a compendium of bad human decision-making and its baleful effects. Indeed, over the course of the book readers learn that people *en masse* are predictably irrational when it comes to all kinds of choice scenarios. This bleak picture of human cognitive capacities is offset, however, by Thaler and Sunstein's almost unflagging sunniness when it comes to the power of social scientific rationality to correct bias and engineer solutions to societal problems. What society needs to overcome the woeful consequences of all these irrational biases is a class of expert social scientists—"choice architects"—who can redesign private and public institutions to promote social well-being. Indeed, the central concept of "nudging" contains within it the notion that social scientific elites benevolently modulate and engineer the behavior of others. A "nudge" is a mechanism of social engineering in which "choice architecture . . . alters people's behavior in a predictable way without forbidding any options or significantly changing their economic incentives."[6]

While Thaler and Sunstein are absolutely clear that all humans suffer from biases and need nudging, they also are consistent in their inference that social scientific elites are a privileged class that can design nudges for everyone else ("choice architects"). Indeed, there is an entire rhetorical dimension to Thaler and Sunstein's book that involves constructing themselves and their readers as technocratic subjects, dictating policy, and the masses of "people" as nudge-able objects ("powerful nudges . . . must be selected with caution" they warn, like sorcerers instructing the apprentice).[7]

Throughout Thaler and Sunstein's book there is a sense that the majority of people are only marginally capable of self-rule because they consistently embody the automatic, biased, irrational aspects of the brain. We are told, for example, that "voters . . . rely primarily on their Automatic System"; that "people tend to be somewhat mindless, passive decision makers"; and that they "accept questions as posed" because they are too "busy and have limited attention."[8] By contrast, although also mired in the same cognitive biases, a technocratic elite is able to momentarily overcome these limitations for the sake of constructing rational, scientific public policy that promotes social harmony. In other words, social scientists (and presumably the readers of *Nudge*) have a privileged ability to exit the automatic mind. After all, they are the ones with the specialized knowledge of cognitive psychology and behavioral economics. There is an implied form of class hierarchy in terms of who is able to exit the "automatic" brain to formulate public policy and who is predominantly nudge-able, living out political life on autopilot.

To be clear, Thaler and Sunstein affirm that social engineering should only be used with a light touch and in a way that promotes goals selected by ordinary people. They maintain that individual voters (the people) choose the ends of political life. This is what they call their "libertarian" commitment to freedom and individual choice. However, after selecting a broad value, policy preference, or candidate, the actual work of governing is carried out by an elite representative class of professional "choice architects."

This worldview fits well with a version of "democracy" in which heightened inequality absorbs the majority of ordinary people in simply trying to economically survive, as political participation is reduced to periodic voting for a broad platform or a candidate. What is ruled out by Thaler and Sunstein's notion of nudging is a society in which everyone is given a chance to develop the educational resources and leisure to exit the automatic mind. Indeed,

Thaler and Sunstein never even consider that exit from automatic mind would be better achieved by radically increased leisure for ordinary people and local control of civic spaces. Instead, their political theory is unreflectively technocratic and their vision of democracy one in which a few elites are given resources to overcome their biases (and everyone else's biases for them). In other words, Thaler and Sunstein appear to be scientifically describing a cognitive problem, when they are in fact helping to reinforce a highly hierarchical form of democracy in an age of inequality.

Reading their book from this perspective unveils a persistent Neoplatonic view of political society, one in which the masses of common people are for the most part associated with the automata of the lower brain, and the technocrats embody the high, rational brain. Although Plato's vision of the soul and polity was tripartite, there is an analogous class structure at play in Thaler and Sunstein's dualistic schema. Indeed, the entire book could be read as a modern version of Plato's city-soul analogy: just as the human mind has a hierarchical cognitive architecture, so too is society ruled by a cognitive elite. Of course, in stark contrast to Plato's cosmic account of the wisdom of philosopher-kings, Thaler and Sunstein instead vaunt the findings of behavioral economics and cognitive science, empowering social science technocrats who quietly sit on the throne of power. Yet similar to Plato's *Republic*—which weighs everything from what citizens will eat for dessert (figs) to whom they will breed with (only those philosophers allow)—once this benevolent elite is in power, no social space is too minute or trivial to be left to democratic control. In the course of *Nudge* everything from reducing urinal "spillage" in public bathrooms to redesigning retirement plans is considered. Given that *Nudge* was written during President Barack Obama's tenure and that one if its authors (Sunstein) went on to become a chief adviser in his administration, the book might be read as a looping double-H effect, justifying and enacting rule by Ivy League technocrats.

Indeed, in a period that saw precipitous growth in inequality, the bailing out of banking elites, and mass civic frustration, Thaler and Sunstein may have played a role in creating a hermeneutic feedback loop for America's educated classes. Because the demos were said to be too "busy," "passive," and "mindless" to exit their automatic brains, public policy that tried to correct the social and economic conditions of such a state of affairs largely disappeared from the agenda in favor of cleverer ways for technocrats to design everyone else's civic spaces for them. *Nudge* can thus partly be read as an artifact of class privilege and how social science elites at the beginning of the twenty-first century claimed to have the leisure and intelligence to overcome their own cognitive biases (at least while formulating public policy) while everyone else was too busy enduring a radically unequal America.

The foregoing analysis suggests that much of popular social science in its various, competing theoretical instantiations may be read as expressive of a particular kind of modern ethical self, one that is technocratic and manipulative in its dealings with others. This technocratic, managerial self is achieved by ignoring and distorting culture in favor of a supposedly scientific idiom. Or perhaps more accurately, technocrats do not ignore meanings but rather confuse the creation of one set of meanings with the basic, official, and authoritative findings of science. Many people who believe they are doing science are in fact doing ideology; they are making meanings and involved in the art of interpretation.

Indeed, as Deirdre McCloskey pointed out many years ago in the case of economics, there is an entire repressed poetics in the major writings of social science. Because we are inescapably meaning-making creatures, the only way for the "science" of such writers to take effect within the ordinary world is if they create meanings for us to inhabit. The technical jargon itself is part of this creative act but can only go so far in generating a new social reality. A persuasive exhortation and poeticizing is also necessary. In this vein, there is something strangely entrancing and poetic in Thaler and Sunstein's entire deployment of the metaphor of a "nudge" and its associated variations (nudging, nudged, nudge-able). Popularizers of neuroscience and cognitive psychology likewise pen rapturous chains of descriptions, and Pinker is perhaps unrivaled in producing incandescent turns of phrase such as "the memory is like a bulletin board"; emotions a "keyboard"; the mind a "spook," an "ethereal nothing"; and the brain "globs of neural tissue" and a "billiard ball clacking."[9]

Of course, for a double-H effect to take place a reader must allow these poetics to enter his or her own self-interpretations and self-understandings. When absorbing popular pieces of social science, as with any work of literary fiction, there is a moment of suspended disbelief as the meanings take hold. The result is a world in which an ethos of scientific manipulation has assumed greater power and ideological authority, without ever straightforwardly making the moral or political case for itself. As readers look around and see increasingly computerized dating practices or the common person taking on several jobs or struggling to plan for retirement, a feedback loop of meanings is created. The theory appears confirmed by the very reality it culturally and politically helps spawn.

The portrait of this society of scientific manipulation still requires more development. For now one lesson is that social science makes a very long and strange descent from the peaks of high academic theory into the valleys of mass culture. In its high-genre form, social science appears disembodied on an academic journal page, technical in its jargon, third person in its perspective, and free of any ideological or ethical taint. However, as this discourse migrates into the popular arena, it takes on more accessible, poeticized, and overtly ideologized meanings. While the high-genre academic monograph kept to a rhetoric of dry rigor, the vulgarized form often openly and crassly declares the underlying metaphor in all its brutality.

Social science has yet to come to terms with this strange metamorphosis of high theory into ethical and ideological enactments. If it could it would recognize that there are always complex ethical and political features grafted into the meanings generated by social scientific theories. This implies that it is possible to object to the meanings of social science theories at least partly on ethical grounds. The question always remains open: Ought I to become even more like this or that social scientific theory? Ought I to actively embody it, growing in awareness of its ramifications and letting it become a deeper part of who I am? Do I use social science to build a new world and a new me?

PART III

Scientific Violence

Sciences of Zero Tolerance

In 2014 thousands of people watched Internet footage of Eric Garner dying in full daylight under a New York City police officer's chokehold. Garner, a grandfather and former city employee, was suspected of selling "loosies" or individual cigarettes, a popular item in poor neighborhoods, where taxes had rendered tobacco products increasingly unaffordable. A burly black man who suffered from asthma, Garner could be clearly heard gasping "I can't breath" eleven times as Officer Daniel Pantaleo pinned him to the sidewalk and other officers crowded around. The dramatic disproportion between crime and enforcement shocked viewers as the video went viral and spurred a tense nationwide debate.

Why had Officer Pantaleo reacted to a minor infraction of the law with such swift and overwhelming force? Why had the surrounding police officers treated his response as a matter of course? Some claimed the incident was an isolated mishap, but others saw a disturbing pattern of police brutality against black men. Few realized that a significant factor leading to the death of Eric Garner involved popular social scientific authority and

its restructuring of the political world. Decades before Garner's
death, scientism had revamped the dominant mode of American
policing.

   This chapter investigates how social scientific authority has
been used to justify domination and violence. Beginning in the
1970s and 1980s, social science theories played a vital role in
transforming police tactics from a rehabilitative model to the
current paradigm of "zero tolerance" and "law and order." While
presenting itself as the officially rational, objective, and scientific
way of conducting law enforcement, this form of policing is in
fact linked to an increasingly militarized and racialized politics.
This remains unrecognized because many people still implicitly
adhere to their perception of society as something like sociologist
Max Weber's view of a single, homogenous, rationalized modernity. The world we live in materializes not as one possible culture among many but as the sole, inescapable form of scientific
society.

IMAGINING LAW AND ORDER

Declarations of the discovery of a science supporting law enforcement are not new. On the contrary, the very origins of criminology as a field of study came from an intellectual movement in
1800s Europe that claimed crime was not chiefly a moral or political problem but a scientific one. A crucial pioneer in this movement was Cesare Lombroso. Lombroso believed some people
were born criminals and could be identified by unique physiological markers—like the slope of the forehead, shape of the
jaw, and physique—that supposedly linked them to a throwback,

primitive subhuman.[1] Lombroso's co-option of biological and evolutionary language played a role in authorizing racial hierarchy during the nineteenth century, such as in the creation of Jim Crow America and its obsession with the "Negro problem."[2]

However, the theorists who helped build and imagine the science undergirding zero-tolerance policing did not accept Lombroso's crudely biological suppositions. Instead, they drew on various late-twentieth-century social science theories, including rational choice and behavioral genetics. Key leaders of this intellectual movement were political scientists James Q. Wilson and Charles Murray, psychologist Richard Herrnstein, and criminologist George Kelling. These researchers built an elaborate social scientific apparatus out of ostensibly color-blind concepts and a rhetoric of unsentimental willingness to follow wherever the data led.

The main nemesis of these law-and-order scholars was the rehabilitative approach to crime championed during the American New Deal. New Deal social democrats had thought of crime as part of a wider constellation of problems such as economic inequality, educational gaps, and social isolation. New Dealers thus tended to be pessimistic about the impact of policing on crime rates and stressed the coordinated action of government across many spheres.[3] By contrast, the ascendant law-and-order social scientists saw these approaches as naively implicated in the cycle of crime by being too soft on lawbreakers. Wilson, Murray, and their confederates wished to see politicians "get tough" on crime by turning police, prisons, prosecutors, and criminal justice into the chief (if not exclusive) tools of crime fighting. They thus envisioned society as a dualistic war between law-abiding citizens and criminals. Indeed, Murray even announced that when "imprisonment numbers . . . started to soar" in the United States in the 1980s, this was a sign of scientific progress.[4]

How popularized social scientific authority helped enact this new world—constituting an insidious double-H effect—can be examined along three converging lines. Consider first what was popularly imagined as the "broken windows" approach to policing. Grasping this point requires some background. Wilson and Herrnstein—in their seminal 1985 book, *Crime and Human Nature*—employed economic rational choice methods to conceive of crime through the metaphor of markets. This allowed them to imagine all criminals as a species of *Homo economicus*: rationally calculating complex ratios of cost-benefit to determine whether a given crime was worth the price. The policy prescription inferred from this theory was that lawmakers needed to ensure the cost of criminal behavior was so high that overwhelming numbers of people would come to the conclusion that such actions were unprofitable. Wilson and Herrnstein were thus methodologically committed to the notion that criminal behavior was "rational" in the narrow sense of strategic, egoistic, and preference maximizing. "It is a mistake," they cautioned readers, "to argue about whether a given offense is or is not 'rational.'"[5]

This purely abstract and fictive conception of criminal psychology as economic in nature had a number of consequences for the world of policing. For one thing, it critically worked against those who claimed education, welfare, and other forms of rehabilitation needed to be part of combatting crime. It claimed that such approaches risked tipping a would-be criminal's calculus in favor of lawbreaking by being too lenient. After all, Wilson and Herrnstein had imagined individuals as constantly haggling over the cost of criminal action like shoppers in search of deals.

Society must therefore maintain a constant police presence and enact harsh, forceful punishments, even publicly if need be to predictably neutralize the ever-present threat of delinquency.

This social scientific conception of crime, in popularized form, helped spawn perhaps the most influential policing strategy of the last half century. "Broken windows" policing tellingly began life in 1982 as a popular article in the *Atlantic*. Wilson, now with his coauthor George Kelling, suggested that toleration of petty crimes (e.g., vandalism, panhandling, loitering) raised the chances that individuals would commit serious offenses (e.g., assault, larceny, homicide). In their famous image, a neighborhood that tolerated small acts of vandalism such as broken windows would predictably experience higher rates of violent crime. Small infractions were thus "inextricably linked" to grave breaches of law because "one unrepaired broken window is a signal that no one cares, and so breaking more windows costs nothing."[6]

With this turn of phrase, Wilson and Kelling made an imaginative leap and articulated perhaps the most enduring symbol of American crime in a generation. The conjuring of an urban neighborhood full of broken windows had a massive, bewitching effect, a rhetorical device supposedly unlocking the secrets of a deep science. Like many powerful acts of imagination, the symbol of broken windows gave millions of people a new way of organizing reality. Suddenly the fear that small infractions might lead to a crime wave was not paranoid, pusillanimous, or authoritarian. On the contrary, it was clear-headed, rational, and scientific.

This was accepted because society was believed to be structured by a crime market. All infractions of law—no matter how small—altered the prices on this market and changed the calculus of potential criminals: the homeless person sleeping in the park, the impoverished teen jumping a turnstile, the men sharing a bottle on the street corner, the grandfather selling loosies. The consequence of tolerating such small misdeeds was an eventual "criminal invasion."[7] Similarly, an all-out war on panhandlers, loiterers, and pilferers was also a war on serious crime like rape, murder, and larceny. According to this view, Eric Garner was not simply a poor man committing a minor infraction. He was a sower of disorder whose persistent and open acts of defiance might pull the entire community into anarchy. This vision—presented to policy makers, citizens, and police officers as part of the basics of criminology—unsurprisingly led to a crisis of the continual excessive use of force. Indeed, was any force against such sowers of disorder really too much? This brutally dark vision of enforcement under the pseudoscientific moniker of "broken windows" became the official approach to policing in New York City under Mayor Rudolph Giuliani; later it was adopted by many cities nationwide.

Legal theorist Bernard Harcourt has masterfully explored the ways in which this concept of "disorder"—although officially color-blind—had de facto racist consequences when put into practice. After all, as police enacted the social scientific theories of Wilson, Kelling, and Herrnstein, "disorder" was interpreted as present in some infractions at the expense of others. Many of the minor crimes treated as problematic had unspoken racial and class dimensions. For example, common infractions associated with the whiter upper class (e.g., illegally hiring a landscaper or worker, tax evasion, jaywalking, serving alcohol to minors at a private party) were considered more tolerable and not truly disordered. By contrast, the minor infractions associated with poorer, browner people (e.g., selling loosies, sharing drinks on the stoop, jumping turnstiles) were unacceptable and scientifically linked to a crime wave. As Harcourt brilliantly observed: "Our modern conception of the disorderly" was "an unattached, young, most often racialized other, with a powerful tendency to commit crime."[8] The fundamental claim to an empirics of disorder was in fact an entire interpretive grid with repressed racial, economic, and ideological meanings.

A perpetual war on crime waged on poorer, browner communities was in turn a major driver of the mass-imprisonment phenomenon in the United States, which jails a larger percentage of its citizens (and racial minorities) than any other country on Earth. These double-H effects helped create a world in which, as Michelle Alexander has shown, black men are subject to incarceration rates for drug charges "twenty to fifty times greater than those of white men" despite similar levels of infraction.[9] Popular social science had thus helped intellectually launder a new kind of racial hierarchy, one in which truly "disordered" people were punished in a way supposedly justified by criminological theory.

This brings me to a second social scientific theme articulated by this cadre of theorists that helped inaugurate a new political reality. This theme emphasized not the market-like aspects of criminality but the behavioral inputs. Here the social scientific sources came from behavioral psychology, which presented humans as conditioned by external factors (genetics, family life, social structure, etc.) and not as economic rationalists. The behavioristic part of Wilson and Herrnstein's theory was in tension philosophically with the rational choice assumptions of broken windows policy. After all, an agent could not be both acting according to rational economic calculation and determined by basic inputs. This theoretical incoherence was never resolved.

Putting the philosophical puzzles aside, Wilson and Herrnstein's *Crime and Human Nature* advanced this behavioral thesis as the statistical proposition that although certain inputs did not causally destine a person to criminal behavior, such factors could heighten its likelihood. For example, Wilson and Herrnstein suggested that there was a "clear and consistent link between criminality and low intelligence" because "low intelligence will favor impulsive crimes with immediate rewards."[10] Similarly, they hypothesized that inherited and deeply socialized personality traits like assertiveness, risk-taking, unconventionality, and extroversion were strongly correlated with criminality and heightened chances of lawbreaking.

Therefore, although Wilson and Herrnstein insisted that no one was born a criminal (as in Lombroso's crude determinism), enough behavioral inputs combined in a single individual allowed social scientists to posit the existence of high-risk, repeat offenders. As Wilson and Herrnstein put it, "a given individual . . . may be so predisposed to crime that no feasible change in institutionally controlled re-enforcers . . . may make a difference."[11] In other words, for certain individuals—behaviorally overdetermined to criminality—no societal efforts at education or rehabilitation were worthwhile. Indeed, to launch such efforts was an unrealistic, naïve, and positively harmful dissipation of resources. Empirical science had established that certain people were more or less hopelessly criminal.

In mass culture, such a conception of criminality helped undergird the metaphor of criminals as "predators" and "super predators" popularized by leaders of both parties as part of the zero-tolerance policies of presidents Ronald Reagan and Bill Clinton. "Predator" is, of course, a term borrowed from biology, used to classify animal species whose natural behavior is to kill and consume other animals for survival. In the law-and-order movement, the metaphor of the predator was mobilized to imagine an individual whose behavioral inputs render him (the individual was nearly always male, brown, and poor) irredeemably antisocial and violent. The collective imagining of predators wandering America's city streets animalized racial minorities and suggested individuals so deeply criminal that the only rational policy response was to hunt them. Indeed, police needed to become hunters of natural hunters, availing themselves of the latest weaponry and military training. As Senator Joseph Biden recommended in a speech to Congress in 1993: with "predators on our streets," Americans have "no choice but to take them out of society."

Taken to their logical conclusion, such behavioristic theories of crime recommended total incapacitation. Even small infractions were potential flags indicating probabilistic inputs that were more nefarious. In societies of high racial and class animus, these social scientific claims easily translated into political despair over and loathing of entire demographic categories of people (black, Latino, immigrant, etc.). The policy response was a form of criminal justice aimed at permanently pulling out of society as many potential predators as possible through harsh mandatory minimum sentencing laws, strict probation regimes, mass incarceration, and indefinite internment camps. If society was menaced by super predators, then the rational response was an enormously complex system of walled communities—both public and private—and cages dividing the law-abiding from the lawbreaking.

A final double-H effect worth noting that sprang from the scientism of the super predator was the justification for a much more thorough militarization of the police. The undisputed pioneer in tracking the dramatic militarization of American police forces is criminologist Peter Kraska. Kraska spent years tracing a radical transformation in American police training, equipment, and culture as they shifted from a citizen, democratic model to a highly militaristic, authoritarian approach. This was evident, for instance, in the spread of special weapons and tactics (SWAT) units among local police forces in the 1980s and 1990s as well as the way that America's ghettos were increasingly policed with war technologies and a "counterinsurgency, low intensity conflict model."[12] In other words, policing America's poor neighborhoods was not seen as a collaborative project carried out between government and citizens but as the patrolling of a war zone. Given this militarized, scientistic culture, it is unsurprising that in the United States police during this time regularly killed more people in a day than other countries did in years. Indeed, one study found that England and Wales (both with far more democratized, unarmed policing cultures) had only fifty-five fatal police shootings in the twenty-four *years* leading up to 2015, while the United States had fifty-nine fatal police shootings in the first twenty-four *days* of 2015.[13] The discrepancy between number of blacks and Latinos versus whites killed was also enormous. One black father in Los Angeles, whose son was shot to death by the police, sadly confessed to a reporter: "It's like they got some kind of mandate to kill our black young men."[14]

The racialized, authoritarian, and militarized dimensions of this massive shift in policing culture did not register within the paradigm's own self-understanding. Instead, the notion that police tactics were scientifically rational was increasingly expressed in a style that vaunted technological advancement and control. In his ethnographies, Kraska described a militarized policing subculture with its "cold, fearless, mechanistic look," "Kevlar helmets," "wraparound sunglasses," "futuristic style," and robotic "techno-warrior image."[15] In this way, the culture of scientism had led to a shift in police aesthetics toward futurism. With super predators supposedly wandering open, hostile urban environments (impervious to dialogue, education and economic incentives), foot soldiers would need to be deployed with the latest military technologies. What the futuristic Robocop aesthetic communicated was a technocratic fantasy of scientifically inflicted violence. What the guillotine was to the French Revolution, the SWAT unit became to early twenty-first-century America.

ENACTING RACIAL PROFILES

A final way popular social science helped inaugurate the new technocratic police power was through an openly racialized route. In 1985 Wilson and Herrnstein had suggested that race and other biological inputs were relevant to statistical criminal tendencies (and I have already noted that several double-H effects had clear racial dimensions once put into practice). But Wilson and Herrnstein also took further the argument that there were basic scientific inputs determining a person's criminal tendencies and tied it specifically to race as a potential empirical indicator of delinquency.

An entire chapter of *Crime and Human Nature* was devoted to race. But whereas most races were treated only in passing, Wilson and Herrnstein focused at considerable length on blacks. Indeed, in the course of the chapter almost no possible source that could be used to insinuate a conception of blacks as pathological was left untouched, including claims about supposedly lower intelligence, impulsiveness of temperament, broken family life, a tumultuous history, and deviant subculture. Even discredited Lombrosian anatomical classifications (like the supposedly higher tendency of blacks to manifest "heavy-boned muscularity" and "mesomorphic" builds) were revived by Wilson and Herrnstein as potential markers of criminality.[16]

Although Wilson and Herrnstein were careful to treat all their claims as statistical probabilities and not deterministic, the overall message of these passages was unmistakable: blacks presented a composite of genetic, psychological, and cultural inputs that all predisposed them en masse to greater criminality. This was a subtle revival in social scientific discourse of the nineteenth-century "Negro problem" or the claim of insuperable difficulties for the white race in sharing a society with people of African descent. Indeed, Wilson and Herrnstein concluded that all the "theories" they treated correlating blacks with crime were "probably true" and "partially correct."[17]

These racialized social scientific theses would reappear a decade later in Charles Murray and Herrnstein's extraordinarily popular work *The Bell Curve*. Here the claims were presented as part of a discourse on behavioral genetics that claimed to empirically reveal the way in which American class and race hierarchies

reflected basic biological differences. Although behavioral genetics never received full recognition by biologists and geneticists,
it sometimes thrived in the psychology departments of American
universities. But where behavioral genetics truly flourished and
spread was in the nonexpert, popular discourse on everything
from obesity and sexual orientation to race and gender. The press
was frequently ready to announce the latest findings of genetic
determinants of complex human meanings and behaviors.

The sociologist Aaron Panofsky has shown that—although
kept at a distance by mainstream social and natural scientists in
the academy—behavioral genetics nonetheless succeeded in the
public arena in creating a popular, superstitious discourse he
calls "astrological genetics."[18] Astrological genetics is the peculiar modern practice of reading biological signs on human bodies
(said to reveal the genetic code) and determining a particular
individual's or group's fate. Whereas some premodern societies
sought to prophesy individual destinies by reading celestial signs,
scientism inspires an analogous practice of reading the signs of
race, gender, physique, and so on to divine a person's destiny. In
the elaborate scientism of astrological genetics, basic biological
features are said to be causally related to higher identity characteristics such as creativity, intelligence, aggression, athleticism,
musicality, libido, attraction, desire, and so on.

In terms of law-and-order policing, behavioral genetics joined
a much longer tradition of creating the concept of race and seeing
the world through racial categories. In the opening pages of this
book I discussed how the modern concept of race was invented
by mixing concepts from biological taxonomy with social and political elements (biologizing the cultural). What was distinctively
modern about racism in this respect was the belief that one was

peering deep into the human structure by reading the outward, superficial signs of race. This deep structure was supposedly responsible for mechanistically fixing humans into a hierarchy of capacities. As historians have shown, a particularly crude early version of the modern concept of race was born with Linnaeus's taxonomies.

Astrological genetics as a way of reading the superficialities of race to find a deep structure determining criminality is the final way in which popular social science was deployed to construct the new technocratic policing. From an interpretive perspective the phenomenon of race is cultural because it always involves ascribing significance or meaning to physical qualities. People who engage in racial thinking privilege a fundamentally arbitrary subset of biological features (skin tone, structure of the nose, hair, etc.) to read a whole set of social narratives about character, heroes, and villains, in a kind of repressed hermeneutics.

This is one way to understand the enormously important insights of cultural theorist Stuart Hall and his notion that race is a "floating signifier." According to Hall, the perception that a cluster of physical features forms a race is not grounded in biology but is rather a cultural and historical phenomenon. Race as a set of brute biological features is used as a shorthand for reading certain cultural and political histories. This is why reading bodies can lead modern people into such trouble—because reading the physical cues often greatly misleads about the actual identity of the person in question (e.g., the cultural and historical experience of someone from Accra sharing similar biological features to an individual born in Chicago). This is what Hall calls the "trap" of race: when modern people read physical signs and expect them to guarantee the meaning and significance of a particular person's

identity. Racial thinking is a trap because it puts its faith in physical traits as a method for reading cultural, social, and psychological content.

If Hall is right, a huge part of modern racism involves the invention of a pseudoscientific literature, so to speak, for reading
bodies, in which certain physical traits are like letters and symbols.
For this reason, Hall says that "race works like a language. . . . [It]
is closer to how a language works, than of how our biology is or
our physiologies work."[19] This is also why the meaning of race is
constantly changing, being challenged, resisted, imposed, revised,
and debated. It is floating in meaning, which connotes that it can
be reinterpreted and perceived anew. Race constitutes a massive
case of a double-H effect, in which social scientific theories and
a culture of scientism penetrate into social reality, suggesting
that we read certain traits as races. As Hall notes of racialized
societies: "The body is a text and we are all readers of it."[20]

Hall's interpretive discussion of race implies that the law-and-
order theorists were never simply describing an empirical reality. In fact, they were participating in an attempt to rewrite the
meaning of certain physical traits. In other words, they (no less
than writers of fiction) were involved in getting us to see race
and racial characteristics as signs or indicators of some deeper
meaning. These biological signs were then ready to be viewed as
part of certain popular ideological narratives. The theorists of law
and order were deep in Hall's trap of race because they assumed
that by correlating physical indicators (dark skin, broad nose,
tightly curled hair, etc.) with certain behavioral propensities (aggression, impulsiveness, etc.), they were simply describing bodies.
In fact, they were proposing a way to read social reality with the
use of physical indicators. Wilson and Murray are ideologists

who believe they are doing science. They have fallen under the spell of their own scientism.

In the realm of policing and law enforcement, their theories implied that bodies could be read, shorthand for a supposed hidden probabilistic code portending greater chances of criminality. A key feature of zero-tolerance policing was the erosion of older American legal norms about search and seizure. In the political world, the spread of practices such as stop-and-frisk and racial profiling were lent the authority of science by those claiming to have unlocked a probabilistic science with the power to predict patterns in human behavior. Donald Trump—who ran as a law-and-order candidate—during his 2016 election defended racial profiling, arguing that if the police "see somebody that's suspicious, they will profile" and that being "politically correct" should not obstruct police from employing this tactic.[21] The claim that political correctness was obstructing the hard, empirical truth of racial bodies was a rhetorical move made decades earlier by Wilson, Herrnstein, Murray, and other popular social scientists. Racial thinking's ultimate moral authority has always been a kind of scientism and expertise, without which it would be dealt a potentially fatal blow.

The most common defense of the law-and-order movement is that—whatever the merits or demerits of the social science that helped create it—police tactics of zero tolerance work. Such tactics, after all, did coincide with a dramatic drop in the crime rate. But the problem with this defense is that it is false. The implementation of law-and-order policing by Giuliani did not in any clear way lead to the lowering of crime in New York City in the 1990s. Later empirical research has raised the question of whether the New York "miracle" under Giuliani was largely a mirage. The research of Harcourt once again has been hugely important, uncovering an extensive case against the attribution of a falling crime rate to zero-tolerance policing. Indeed, Harcourt observed that many American cities that rejected zero tolerance (including Boston, Los Angeles, San Diego, and Houston) also experienced dramatic drops in the crime rate during the same period.[22] Yet this "science" of crime fighting continues to be the intellectual basis for the nationwide call for tougher policing.

The central interpretive point of this chapter is that law and order was not so much discovered as it was imagined and performed. Popular social science has played an unrecognized role in inaugurating this process, as many of its descriptions are in fact imaginings, and many of its imaginings are a script for social performance. What thus resulted from law-and-order theorists was a massive instance of a double-H effect in which what claimed to be empirical social science was actually the articulation and enactment of an ideology.

The mistake once again is to repress the interpretive features of social reality in favor of a supposedly scientific theory. But what if the initial data reflect some particular world of meanings? If this is the case, then democratic societies should openly deliberate over and debate the cultural, ideological, and ethical meanings of their policies and not pretend that certain theories are offering the officially scientific account of human social and moral life. The double-H effects of the penetration of such social scientific theory into political reality show that theories of crime are never straightforwardly neutral. In the case of modern police, what are presented as inescapable social scientific facts are instead the ideological artifacts of a lived social theater called law and order.

Empire of Light

The exercise of religious authority as a justification for violence is a somber, blood-saturated reality of history. Far less frequently detected is the abuse of scientific authority as a distinctively modern way of enacting violence. A culture of pseudoscience generates a particular version of the dichotomy between civilization and barbarism. In this view, the violence of other societies is backward, benighted, and inspired by the delusional scribbling of religious divines. By contrast, the violence of modern societies is scientific; rational; written into the book of nature; and inscribed in high theoretical concepts such as rights, democracy, utility, and reason. The popularization of social science has played a significant role in articulating these abstractions and shaping the modern mythos of rational violence.

A central instance of this marriage of social scientific authority and force is evident in the culture surrounding the American war on terror. President George W. Bush's speeches after September 11, 2001 (9/11)—justifying the invasions of both Afghanistan and Iraq—are peppered with allusions to one of the most prestigious findings of political science: democratic peace theory, or the hypothesis that democracies rarely if ever engage in military conflict with one another. For example, when rallying troops in Afghanistan in 2006, Bush asserted that "history has taught us democracies don't war" and "democracies yield the peace," because "you don't run for office in a democracy and say, please vote for me, I promise you war."[1]

Putting aside the irony that Bush ran for a second term as president on the basis of his ability to prosecute the war on terror, a vulgarized form of political science had helped furnish a justification for global military intervention and regime change. Astonishingly for a discipline that often chastised itself for its irrelevance to public policy, here its research was being evoked to support the most fateful war effort in a generation. In fact, a popularized form of political science was doing nothing less than helping ordinary citizens picture the need to exercise violence in countries thousands of miles away that most could not even locate on a map.

Adding to the paradoxical nature of the war on terror was the fact that this war—with no traditional territorial foe, defeatable on a field of battle—was initiated at a time when the United States had achieved unprecedented military dominance. As historian Daniel Immerwahr has extensively chronicled, after World War II the United States largely gave up a traditional colonial empire and instead built an elaborate international system of military bases. This was a new form of power that Immerwahr, following historian Bill Rankin, calls a "pointillist empire," in which the globe was influenced militarily through a small network of points. Gone were the land grabs of prior empires. In their place fortified bases perched on foreign soil housed the latest military technologies at the ready (computerized drones, nuclear warheads, next-generation fighter jets), able to project power over every other region on Earth. In total the United States had approximately eight hundred such bases, while the other nations of the world combined possessed about thirty.[2]

There was therefore a tension at the center of the American war on terror. On the one hand, the United States was a nonaggressor state, an anti-imperial defender of democracy taking no unprovoked action against other nations and respecting the sovereign will of the people in its fight to eradicate "terror" wherever it was found. On the other hand, it ran a vast, deterritorialized empire of military bases able to threaten any perceived foe with annihilation (nuclear or otherwise). In other words, it governed the world through occasional acts of military might meant to induce a psychological threat (even terror). How could the leading champion of anti-imperial freedom and foe of terror at the same time control the vastest, mightiest empire on Earth through a psychology of implied threats?

American social scientists working during this period offered various theories that served as ideological resolutions to this paradox. In broad strokes, the United States was depicted as exercising force in a different, enlightened form. Its state-sponsored violence and global system of threats were not aggressive but represented a rational, even scientific type of peacekeeping. In other words, acts such as invading Afghanistan, setting up nuclear warheads in Europe, building offshore torture cells in Guantanamo, and actively seeking to topple governments in Latin America operated as a kind of optical illusion. Viewed through the eyes of popular social science, such violence was in fact peaceful, rational, and terror-free. A vulgarized form of scientific authority thus helped ordinary people envision the United States as an un-imperial, even anti-imperial empire. In this way scientific authority made another long descent, this time away from high academe and into the rhetoric of US presidents, where democracies never conquered, dominated, or terrorized other countries but simply aided in their achieving freedom.

THE PERPETUAL WAR FOR PERPETUAL PEACE

The story of the alignment between the war on terror and social scientific authority goes back a few decades. In the 1980s and 1990s, a popular political discourse in North Atlantic societies emerged that was dominated by a sense of triumph around individual rights, laissez-faire markets, and democracy. This discourse was lent further credibility by the sudden and completely unforeseen collapse of the Soviet Union. In a short period of time an entire research program of Sovietology and numerous institutes devoted to its study were rendered obsolete. Glasnost, perestroika, the revolutions of 1989, and the demise of the Soviet Union—social science expertise had once again failed to predict the politically defining events of an era.

In the confusion that followed, a swaggering proclamation of liberal democracy and capitalist free markets took control of public debate. Social scientists wishing to articulate the zeitgeist also rushed into the fray. Most famous in this genre was the political scientist Francis Fukuyama, whose book *The End of History and the Last Man* expanded on a short and widely read article published in 1989. In his book Fukuyama proclaimed that liberal democracy (of which the United States was the most powerful defender) was the "endpoint of mankind's ideological evolution," "the final form of human government" that "could not be improved on" because it "satisfied" humankind's "deepest and most fundamental longings."[3]

Fukuyama's argument was based on the assumption that history was determined by a fixed set of developmental stages from primitive to modern society. As he put it, "There is a fundamental process at work that dictates a common evolutionary pattern for all human societies . . . in the direction of liberal democracy."[4] In Fukuyama's telling this process was a complex economic and moral one involving technological innovation and also a dialectic of political recognition. But what captured the popular imagination was not the nuances of Fukuyama's hundreds of pages of analysis but his basic metaphor of human society as participating in an evolutionary mechanics (what Fukuyama called a "directional Mechanism") leading to what could be identified by social scientific reason as the terminus of history.

Indeed, scientific reason not only revealed history's basic workings, it also provided the model of objective progress, which helped serve as an analogy for the triumph of liberal democracy. "The Mechanism that gives history its directionality," Fukuyama wrote, was evident in science, which "builds upon itself" and is "unequivocally cumulative."[5] The citizens of liberal democracies could therefore imagine themselves as involved in a process akin to the advancement of science. Just as scientists made progress in knowledge over many generations, so citizens of liberal democracies participated in the massive task of advancing the objective superiority of their political institutions and way of life on the global stage. A reader of Fukuyama's writings could therefore picture himself or herself as akin to the community of scientific researchers: enlightened, intellectually honest, and hard working in the service of truth. But where scientists produced a body of theoretical knowledge, these citizens gave birth to the highest, final society.

In America of the 1990s and early 2000s, such a line of reasoning suggested that the country's nearly unceasing military engagements, its unrivaled nuclear arsenal, and its unprecedented global basing system were not acts of imperial aggression but part of an evolutionary process of enlightenment. Indeed, although Fukuyama later distanced himself from Bush and the war on terror, he began as an enthusiastic supporter. On September 20, 2001 (just days after the attacks on New York's World Trade Center), Fukuyama joined neoconservative intellectuals in writing a public letter to the president expressing enthusiastic support for his policy of "whipping terrorism"; calling for increased military spending; advocating "military action in Afghanistan"; and insisting on an armed confrontation with Saddam Hussein, who constituted "one of the leading terrorists on the face of the Earth."[6] The administration took notice of such fulsome support, and Fukuyama was named by executive order to a small group of Bush's policy intelligentsia operating under the scientistic title "Council on Bioethics."

Fukuyama's status as a high-profile political scientist, now exalted by the sitting president, symbolically communicated the marriage of social scientific authority and military might. Although such a conclusion was rejected by Fukuyama (who insisted on his preference for the European Union's internationalism), at the time it appeared as though resistance to American foreign policy was also recalcitrance in the face of scientific authority. An unspoken message of this scientistic communion with power was that American wars abroad were the embodiment of rationality. Bush, through his campaigns in the Middle East, was simply advancing the evolutionary arc of history.

Of course Fukuyama was far from the only political scientist whose theories helped lend authority to the war on terror. Bush had explicitly drawn on the authority of democratic peace theory, revived in the early 1980s by Michael Doyle, a Harvard-trained political scientist. Retooling Kant's famous argument of a perpetual peace among republics, Doyle's contribution was to revamp the thesis as principally an empirical claim about modern liberal democracies. Doyle argued that it was a matter of verifiable fact that liberal democracies tended to build a growing "zone of peace" internationally.[7] After the fall of the Soviet Union, large numbers of political scientists turned Doyle's thesis into a research program, with influence extending into political science programs across the country. By the time the war on terror launched, countless American undergraduates had been taught that democratic peace theory constituted a major finding in the scientific study of politics.

For the most part, democratic peace theorists maintained a careful empirical tone that contrasted sharply with Fukuyama's metaphysical speculations about history. Nonetheless, Doyle's classic essay did end with a dramatic effort at forecasting the future of human history. Extrapolating from the growing number of liberal democracies over the prior two centuries, Doyle predicted world peace might break out as soon as 2101 or 2113 as virtually all countries underwent a democratic regime change. "International peace is not a utopian ideal," Doyle concluded, "the natural evolution of world politics and economics . . . drive mankind inexorably toward peace."[8] In this way, two decades before the war on terror political science was already helping its readers imagine an international system in which all societies were re-made roughly along the lines of America's liberal institutions. Moreover, this was presented by Doyle not as a visionary utopia but as a sober fact of science.

Of course, in stark contrast to Bush's later rhetoric, Doyle spent considerable energy arguing that liberal states were as prone as other forms of government to war with nonliberal states. Indeed, many of Doyle's warnings ran directly against Bush's applica-tion of the theory. For instance, he argued strenuously that lib-eral values could themselves be the cause of increased aggression and imperial expansion. So Doyle warned that "confusion, drift, costly crusades, spasmodic imperialism" were all the "record of liberal foreign policy outside the liberal world."[9]

Clearly there was a massive contradiction between Bush's popularized takeover of democratic peace theory and its original, far more complex articulation by Doyle. Nonetheless, democratic peace as a theory existing in the actual political world faced a problem similar to that of twentieth-century Marxism: whether popularizers of a highly nuanced social theory (e.g., Stalin, Bush) were betraying it or revealing certain tendencies when putting it into practice. Doyle's strict technical analysis strongly conflicted with Bush's policies. But at the level of social scientific theory as an imaginative, cultural act, Doyle's science-inspired vision was the more politically potent feature. In other words, like Marx be-fore him, Doyle may have ultimately been more influential as the inadvertent creator of a cultural and ideological imaginary than as an expositor of a science.

In this way, the constellation of meanings known as demo-cratic peace theory escaped the hands of its creators and helped a populace imagine itself as uniquely engaged in rational, scientific

warfare. In fact, not only was America's liberal, free-market democracy scientifically superior at creating peaceful orders, but
it also controlled a clean, futuristic arsenal for exercising force.
Bush's top military officials spoke of a new, historically unprecedented form of warfare whose targets were "not a country, but
a GPS coordinate" and promised "immaculate warfare: pre-
cise strikes, few civilian casualties, and above all, no occupying
armies."[10]

An important part of the culture of scientism enveloping the
war on terror was the American military's increased use of un-
manned drones and metadata to conduct targeted killing. Drones
were navigated remotely by computer operators (as if in a virtual reality video game) and used metadata from cell phones and
social networks to pinpoint enemy combatants. In popular discourse, this new method of warfare offered large swaths of the
public a futuristic imaginary of violence as victimless and clean.
An entire discourse of mathematical and technological precision
thus obfuscated deeper moral and ethical questions about drone
algorithms, incursions into sovereignty, and "collateral damage."
All these were increasingly understood as technical glitches and
not moral-political problems.[11]

In one of the stranger examples of a double-H effect, this new
kind of warfare could be orchestrated by policy elites with full
assurance from the outset that they were not in fact engaged in a
war by the strict scientific definition offered in many versions of
democratic peace theory. On the contrary, political scientists had
defined wars as dyadic conflicts between states that had to reach
certain thresholds of casualties to register empirically. But since
this new form of warfare targeted GPS-identified terrorist cells
and not territorialized states, the war on terror could potentially

be conducted in perpetuity in foreign countries and inside liberal democracies themselves without ever breaking the postulates of liberal peace or counting as a counterexample of their unique peacebuilding capacities.

The war on terror was in this way no war at all, but a way of waging peace. If in the future a liberal democracy were to turn on itself, increasingly targeting citizens, this too might be made to fit within the formal boundaries of liberal peace's conceptual apparatus. After all, the Bush administration had legally argued that the internment of enemy combatants without the basic right of habeas corpus was justified by the war on terror. Perhaps one day in the future the war on terror would be conducted on society itself, with citizens selectively identified as enemy combatants. None of this contradicted democratic peace theory as long as certain basic institutional markers of democracy were still intact.[12] The war on terror—almost by scientific fiat—would not appear on the objective register of military violence and bellicosity. Peace among the liberal democracies, after all, was already perpetual.

CIVILIZATION CRUSADERS

Not all social scientists working in the late twentieth century shared the optimism of Doyle or the intoxicating, metaphysical triumphalism of Fukuyama. In fact, Fukuyama's own teacher, the Harvard political scientist Samuel Huntington, spent the same period arguing against the idea that liberal society was universal and inexorably bound for a peaceful final order. Huntington instead claimed that human life was torn by rival civilizational identities that vied for supremacy in a hostile and sometimes even bloody competition.

For Huntington the existence of civilizations was a basic, empirical fact of social science. As he wrote in his hugely influential 1993 article on the "clash of civilizations," humans were subdivided into basic identity blocs of "civilization consciousness" that were "defined both by common objective elements" such as language, history, and religion as well as "the subjective self-identification of people."[13] The world in its current phase was carved up into eight massive civilizational blocs: Western, Islamic, Confucian, Japanese, Hindu, Slavic-Orthodox, Latin American, and African. Although Huntington allowed for some mixing of civilizations into hybrids, he nonetheless insisted that civilizations were the highest form of cultural identity, intensely felt and above which existed no other. He then suggested that the future of global conflict would occur over "differences among civilizations" that were "not only real" and "basic" but "the product of centuries" and "far more fundamental than differences among political ideologies and political regimes."[14]

Huntington thus offered readers a starkly different imaginary than the one inspired by Fukuyama and democratic peace theorists. Where the latter allowed readers to imagine the international order as a bipolar division between liberal democracies and everyone else, Huntington instead posited multiple civilizational contestants. And where democratic peace theorists foresaw the triumph of a universal liberal creed (under which one day we would all more or less be liberals), Huntington imagined the world as permanently fragmented into a violent mosaic. Indeed, a reader of Huntington's article in the United States and Europe was invited to imagine himself or herself not as part of any universal creed (political, religious, or otherwise) but as a member of a completely siloed civilization. This inescapable disconnect from other people globally, moreover, was presented not as an ideological claim but as a descriptive fact.

Undoubtedly Huntington's way of imagining the world would have been implausible for much of the twentieth century, during which the most violent conflicts had been between nations that supposedly shared a civilization and often among competing claims to a universalistic ideology. Indeed, Huntington's entire conception of civilization was incapable of sustaining the varieties and anomalies of the human past. The basic problem was that civilizations such as "the West" were not homogenous unifiers of human identity but rather contained various incompatible religious, ideological, and cultural traditions. Indeed, the tradition of claiming a "Western" identity was itself a single, historically contingent ideological movement within particular societies and not a marker enveloping them in their totality.

Nonetheless, Huntington's imaginary (which could make no sense of the two world wars or the Cold War) became a highly useful and evocative metaphor for the war on terror. To say that two civilizations were facing off—one Islamic and the other Western—became highly useful as the Bush administration, along with British prime minister Tony Blair, scrambled to build a coalition with other, reluctant European nations. Specifically, Huntington's ideas offered those who had experienced the trauma of 9/11 a supposedly scientific theory of what the violence meant. Throughout his essay, Huntington had characterized the divide between the West and Islam as particularly deep and violent—a "fault line" that had purportedly "been going on for 1,300 years" and exacerbated by the fact that Islamic civilization had "bloody borders."[15]

In this view, 9/11 offered a confirmation of the empirical thesis that a civilization called "Islam" was on a crash course with a civilization called "the West." Even the armed resistance to the war on terror by what Bush called "evil-doers" could appear as further evidence of the clash of civilization thesis. Thus, a double-H effect took place: conducting the war on terror generated its own justification and corroboration of the social scientific theory. Waging a war on mostly Muslim countries further proved that "they" were uniquely violent and insinuated that members of this religion might be difficult to assimilate into Western societies. Not unlike the "Jewish Question" and "Negro Question" before it, the Muslim Question too was constituted by a pseudoscientific discourse.

In describing the world in this way, Huntington and his readers were partly involved in a performative act. Without saying so explicitly, Huntington was asking readers to envision their own identities through these conceptual categories. A reader of Huntington's tract could be imbibing an empirical theory of social science at one level while also undergoing a deep cultural and identity transformation on another (into a defender of "the West"). To describe these civilizational classifications was therefore to also subtly enact them. Huntington's article was filled with a rhetoric of assurances that civilizations were "real," "meaningful," "objective," "intensely" felt, "crucial," "central," "basic," and "fundamental."[16] But the increasing intensity of civilizational identity was itself partly the product of actively recalibrating one's own meanings and perception of the world. The essay was therefore as much an invitation to "clash" as a description of one.

As a result, the entire grid of global politics and the distinction between friend and foe were redrawn according to the dictates of the war on terror. Suddenly Islam—not the spread of a rival universal ideology (e.g., communism), let alone home-grown terrorists (e.g., white supremacy)—became the major security preoccupation. In other words, Huntington's social scientific output participated in the very "civilization rallying" that he claimed to be simply outlining as a feature of contemporary politics.[17]

Later Huntington's civilizational consciousness would also be deployed against other groups. In another popular essay, Huntington implicitly asked his readers to worry about immigrants from Latin America, who, despite their sharing European and Christian roots, he did not classify as "Western." In 2004's "The Hispanic Challenge," Huntington suggested that Latino immigrants posed an existential threat to American society because they were simply too culturally different (non-white, Catholic, Spanish-speaking) to assimilate. The sheer scale and imminence of the border were said to further exacerbate the problem and vitiate American sovereignty. Huntington's two major anxieties—Muslims abroad and Latinos at home—became ideologically normative for the new Republican Party that was born in 2016. In all of this Huntington as much helped to create a new world as to discover one. He might even be considered one of the first social scientists to articulate the ultranationalist ideology that would later be identified with "Trumpism." The war on terror served as a prologue to this return of ultranationalism.

Not all forms of civilizational crusading on behalf of the war on terror took on Huntington's tone of an elite foreign policy tract with Islam and Latinos as its main foes. Some presented the dichotomies of the war on terror as a split between a radical form of scientific, enlightened secularism and religious irrationalism in general (including both Christianity and Islam). The most prominent example of this movement was a popular form of atheism that began to spread widely on the Internet in the post–9/11 period.

At the forefront of this movement were war-on-terror-hawk Christopher Hitchens and the neuroscientist Sam Harris, but the figure most prone to evoke scientific authority for his position was the Oxford biologist Richard Dawkins. Dawkins had achieved international fame for popularizing a Darwinian account of human life, including the metaphor that humans were "survival machines."[18] However, after 9/11, Dawkins increasingly focused on what he saw as the scientific and social ills of religion.

Specifically, Dawkins believed that Darwinian science revealed that religion was a kind of "mental virus."[19] Dawkins knew that Darwin had not applied his theory to human culture. The problem with doing so was that human societies clearly changed at a rate much faster than evolutionary time. Since historical and cultural time moved far more rapidly than evolutionary adaptations, the latter could not be evoked to explain the former.

Dawkins's resolution to this apparently insoluble problem was to posit an entirely new kind of Darwinian social scientific theory that he dubbed the theory of "memes." Memes were units of culture or information that comprised human mental life, fighting for survival in the hardware of the brain. Although operating according to a logic of Darwinian replication, memes were unlike genes in that they were cultural and not genetic or biological in nature. However, like genes, memes also survived according to how effective they were at multiplying and spreading in a competitive environment (the limited cognitive space of the human brain). The most successful memes were those that colonized human attention and memory.

Although presumably all human social life was explicable in terms of the non-rational mechanism of meme colonization, Dawkins spent the majority of his writings elaborating on memes as a way to criticize religious beliefs. For example, Dawkins claimed that "God" was a meme obscuring difficult questions about reality, religious "celibacy" was a meme inhibiting sexual reproduction while encouraging the mental reproduction of religious ideas, and so forth. All this, of course, was presented as descriptive findings of the science of memes.

Islam was a particular anxiety for Dawkins. His bestselling *The God Delusion*, published in 2006, opened with a passage blaming 9/11 and terrorist violence on the existence of religion and ended with an extended metaphor of enlightenment as an act of violently ripping off a "black burka." The book was filled with examples of the supposed inherent barbarism of religion in general and Islam in particular. What was described was a version of the war on terror that was slightly different than either Fukuyama's or Huntington's popularized theories. Here the standoff was between a uniquely universal, post-religious civilization and premodern theocracy. A radical form of secular atheism would rescue the world from the violence of religious terrorism.

Freeing humans from the colonization of the mind viruses of religion required that all the world's cultures transform into secular, liberal democracies. Indeed, sounding like Fukuyama, Dawkins argued that modern, rational societies had as a matter of empirical fact "inexorably" achieved a "broad liberal consensus" that reflected the workings of a kind of scientific law of

society.[20] "Over the longer timescale," Dawkins wrote, "the pro-
gressive trend is unmistakable and it will continue."[21] Dawkins
even saw the American invasion of Iraq, and what he claimed was
its relatively humane execution, as part of the inexorable march
of secular, liberal democracy.

In Dawkins's grand vision, the world faced a dualistic split
between enlightened liberal atheism and backward authoritarian theism. His call was for a public movement of atheists to
rally and mobilize into an open political bloc against religion.
This suggested that the war on terror should more rightly be
reconceived as a war on religion. In this way, scientific liberalism
became for Dawkins a way to crusade against multiculturalism
in favor of a liberal, scientific monoculture. Once religion had
withered away and disappeared, humans would be free to enjoy
freedom, defined not as serious religious or spiritual pluralism
but as exercising various banal market freedoms.

Dawkins never seriously grappled with the tension between
his avowals of the triumph of liberalism and his decidedly illib-
eral views on the religions constituting nearly every traditional
human culture. Instead, for Dawkins the advent of a liberal, materialist atheism would mean a decline in world violence and
a rise in social harmony. After all, Dawkins noted, "individual
atheists may do evil things," but "they don't do evil things in
the name of atheism," and thus no war had been "fought in the
name of atheism."[22] In other words, a liberal, atheist perpetual
peace was on the horizon. At the same time, the pages of *The God
Delusion* expressed a unique, implicit justification for the war on
terror being waged all around Dawkins as he wrote. While he had
believed he was popularizing the Darwinian science of memes,
he had in fact joined in the construction of a culture for his fellow

humans to inhabit. This was the varied scientistic culture of the war on terror.

In short, a complex matrix of meanings—some in tension, some mutually reinforcing—formed the popular scientism of the most recent global war. In the popular imaginary, social scientific concepts objectively proved that this was really no war at all but rather the scientific exercise of power. Scientific authority of a certain distorted kind thus played the handmaiden to power, and figures ranging from Oxford biologists to Harvard political scientists offered theories for advancing the violence of the early twenty-first century. If radical Islam had its imams and fundamentalist Christianity its pastors, scientific authority too had its popular demagogues. Only this was demagoguery of an unrecognized form, for its proudest rallying cry was: "Science and democracy! Science and civilization!"

Conclusion

Reading Social Science Again

We live inside our theories (or exploded fragments of our theories, or dark, distorted mirrors of our theories) in ways not yet sufficiently acknowledged by social scientists. Theories can hold us captive by generating cultures, and cultures are the medium through which human life is made whole. Society is a large skein of meanings—some religious; some scientific, political, or artistic; and some mysterious and only half perceived—all of them embodied. This is one way of interpreting the significance of the great poet Czeslaw Milosz's image of humans as living inside an "interhuman creation . . . a gigantic cocoon hanging from the branch of a cosmic tree." Later in the same poem, "Inside and Outside," Milosz asks: "Are we not seduced by speech? Oratory, high ideological chanting, philosophies, theories—all of them grafted on excrementalities and exhalations of our bodies."[1]

The dominant conception of social scientific texts continues to be largely disembodied. An unreflective practice of mainstream intellectual culture is that of insisting we read the genre of social scientific writing straightforwardly as an act of description and explanation. As Deirdre McCloskey

noted in the case of economics, an entire poetics and rhetoric is deployed when writing in the social science genre: the
third person is evoked, and objects are perfectly translucent
and quantifiable.[2] As a reader one has the sensation of wandering through the space of Euclidean geometry or perhaps
of an architect's drafting board for modeling buildings. Points
are punctual, lines are straight, and everything is drenched in
light. This is the rhetorical style of science. Yet is such a way
of writing really fully appropriate to the social sciences? Or
should a future, more interpretively sensitive social science
deploy a new style, one that is historically sensitive, locates
and identifies the voice of the author, allows other voices to
speak, and is not afraid to avow a cultural perspective? At
present it seems the vast majority of academic social science slavishly imitates the natural sciences when it comes to
matters of style; indeed, perhaps this might be the only site of
truly successful imitation.

Readership has also been drastically transformed along the
lines of the natural science model. An entire habit of mind, dis-
ciplined mentality, and practice of reading has taken form as a
kind of secular ritual. It's as if we as readers only have license to
read social science in one officially sanctioned way (i.e., as science). But the art of interpreting human behavior opened up by
hermeneutics proposes a completely new, unexpected way of
reading these vast, modern texts. Indeed, what if social science
were read not as a descriptive, empirical genre but as an imaginative, ethically and politically exhortative one instead? What if
the massive output by social scientists was read less like Newton's
Principia and more like the novels of James Joyce or, better yet,
Thomas More's *Utopia*, the *Discourses of Epictetus*, the book of
Genesis, and the *Communist Manifesto*? That is, what if we saw

in all social science a performative feature of culture creation, meaning-making, and world-building?

One operating assumption of the hermeneutic or interpretive tradition is that social science (whatever else it may be) is also always a field of interpretation and cultural meanings. This field of interpretation allows the world to emerge in certain ways and not others. Who or what is a criminal? What is the nature of American power? What is a human being, a citizen, a society? Social science builds and enacts these realities and does not simply find them ready-made for description. The purpose of this book has thus been to evoke a mass realignment in how we read social science. Social science should not be dismissed or jettisoned. Its methods and findings are too valuable to do without. But it must be read again and in a way that does not itself participate in the popular culture of scientism.

One effect of reading in this way is that the line between "high" and "low" social science will not be quite as impermeable and firm as some would like. Both academic and popular social science participate in cultural, ethical, and political movements—although one meets the important demands of a scholarly community and the other those of a readership requiring less methodological reassurances. The foregoing line of thought does not eliminate important distinctions between academia and pop social science; it simply opens up the possibility of reading the entire genre of social science on a spectrum, a bit more like reading Charles Dickens's serial novels while also taking into account the wider nineteenth-century phenomenon of "penny dreadfuls." Literary scholars have long recognized that Dickens's serialized novels—which were more expensive and read by an educated readership—were in a complex relationship with the far cheaper, working-class penny dreadfuls (in fact, many of Dickens's own novels were pirated and vulgarized into penny dreadfuls). This is not to eliminate important distinctions or imply that *Oliver Twist* and *Nicholas Nickleby* are the same in quality or merit as the penny dreadful knockoffs *Oliver Twiss* and *Nickelas Nicklebery*.[3] But like literature, social science can also be located within a wider constellation of meanings and not simply as timeless statements of authoritative, empirical documentation.

Most academic social scientists have steered clear of the half-baked theories often inspired by their own efforts. Forced to explain their reticence to engage this vast reservoir of social theory, many would cite its lack of scientific rigor. Yet what if the central problem of superstitious forms of pop social science was not that they were insufficiently scientific, but rather that they were too literal in their reading of the original imaginative suggestions and metaphors? That is, what if the problem is not primarily lackluster commitment to the models inspired by the natural sciences, but rather a literalism not entirely unlike modern biblical fundamentalism and its fanatically single-minded way of reading scripture? If this is the case, then popular social science often gives us the subtler metaphors and cultural meanings of high theory in a form that is mobilized and actionable by huge populations into the political and social world.

Yet the meaning-making features of social science literature are largely neglected due to a false analogy with the natural sciences. Most social science readers operate on the unexamined assumption that the object they are studying is untouched by the genre they are reading. Humans, however, imbibe the treatises of the social sciences (or their vulgarized variants), which make seismic changes in or leave subtle traces on their own beliefs and behaviors. By contrast, subatomic particles cannot read treatises on quantum mechanics, flowers do not contemplate botany, and chimpanzees do not read the latest theories of primatology.

The deeper problem facing a change in mentality around the social sciences is an outgrowth of what the German hermeneutic philosopher Martin Heidegger called the question concerning technology. For Heidegger, technology was not simply an advanced form of instrument or tool making. Rather, Heidegger insisted that technology at a more fundamental, deeper level was a way of looking at and relating to the world and reality. This way of looking at reality made the creation of technological tools possible. In fact, Heidegger believed the technological way of gazing at reality was what generated the artifacts typical of modern life (technologies like the hydroelectric dam, airplane, and computer).

What is the technological way of perceiving and being in the world? The technological gaze sees and interacts with the world as a field of objects whose energies can be scientifically controlled and released. Although Heidegger believed this way of looking at reality extended deep into the history of ancient Greek and Roman culture, he also thought it achieved a decisive articulation with the natural science revolution, which insisted on one kind of causality (what Heidegger referred to as "causa efficiens" or the impersonal mechanistic causality I have discussed) to the exclusion of all other forms. Especially neglected were beliefs, meanings, and purposes as a form of causality that could not be fixed by antecedent mechanistic conditions. So the technological way of being in the world is one that treats all of reality like a mechanics, like physics, like a machine. In this view, no part of reality is above being manipulated by a science of laws and turned into an instrument. The personal features of reality—meanings, history, narrative, culture—can be put aside. Instead, all of reality appears as what Heidegger famously dubbed "standing-reserves," or perhaps better, resources.[4]

This technological way of being in reality and looking at the world as a bucket of resources is what I have been examining in this book. For the technological gaze, human life in its individual and collective forms is so many resources susceptible to manipulation and nudging. There is an entire ethical and political stance built into the technological gaze, a form of organizing society that is technocratic. Technocrats (whether they be Stalinists or free marketeers, AI aficionados or ultra-Darwinists) see society as resources that can be rationally and scientifically organized according to their expert knowledge.

Just as physics provides theoretical insight for engineers to technologically mold the natural world, so a science of society is said to offer knowledge of the various bundles of energies and resources composing human life. Nature and society both then appear as a grid of objects whose energies must be challenged in a struggle for rational control. As Heidegger put it, "Modern technology is a challenging, which puts to nature the unreasonable demand that it supply energy."[5] The unreasonableness of this technocratic stance originates from the attempt to fully control and order something that may not be fully controllable and orderable. In Heidegger's language, the world is confronted through the "ordering attitude" of "modern physics" and the assumption that all forces are "calculable."[6] This uniquely modern ethical and political disorder has been my sustained object of critique.

For example, in chapter 5 I argued that theories of zero-tolerance policing, like those of Charles Murray, James Q. Wilson, and Richard Herrnstein, are pervaded by worry about how to engineer and control what they believe are hidden criminal energies concealed within individuals. These theorists claim that criminal energies are made visible for technocratic management under certain signs: demographic ("youth," "black," "male," "Latino," "unemployed"), temperamental ("impulsive," "assertive," "unconventional"), physical ("heavy-boned," "muscular"), and psychological ("below average intelligence," "poorly socialized"). Each one of these categories is part of an actuarial, probabilistic account of criminality. In other words, the empirical signs are correlated with mechanistic, causal properties. Yet as is also clear from this list, the entire approach is pervaded by racial thinking and has contributed to the high level of animosity in American society. Specifically, it has fed an agenda of purportedly color-blind, scientific control over what turn out to be disproportionately browner and poorer communities. So the technological gaze helps generate the peculiarly modern mass politics of scientism that we normally refer to as "race." The very notion of race comes to be constructed in part out of pseudo-scientific concepts borrowed from sociology, psychology, criminology, and genetics.

But treating people like standing-reserves or bundles of resources and energy to be unlocked by scientists and engineers reduces their dignity and standing. Here I part company with Heidegger, who took his philosophy in the direction of antihumanism and a darkly reactive politics. Instead, the wider hermeneutic tradition can be seen as an effort to retain the distinctive ethical and ontological value of the human person.

Human beings are not reducible to the technological gaze, because they are different within the order of objects in the cosmos. In other words, the interpretive insights of Heidegger actually point back in the direction of humanism. As Heidegger's most important student, Hans-Georg Gadamer, recognized, "the chief task" of interpretive and hermeneutic philosophy in the realm of politics is to guard humanity "against the domination of technology based on science . . . the idolatry of scientific method and the anonymous authority of the sciences."[7]

Human agency is unique from an interpretive perspective because it embodies narratives. That is, human life actually materializes in flesh-and-bone stories, histories, and meanings. As I have been examining all along, this implies that social scientific findings and strictly empirical theories can enter into and be grafted onto the stories that comprise human social and political reality.

That human beings embody stories in this way is a case that has been advanced by many hermeneutic philosophers, including Paul Ricoeur, Charles Taylor, Alasdair MacIntyre, and Gadamer. But it is also a point corroborated by recent psychologists such as Dan McAdams, who heads a broad research program focusing on how healthy humans spontaneously form what he calls a "narrative psychology" or "life-story" as part of maturation. One of McAdams's fundamental findings is that stories are not just aesthetic or cultural add-ons, but rather are vitally necessary to the human psychological process of personal integration. Without stories human identity disintegrates. Indeed, some of the most difficult transitions in human life (e.g., adolescence, midlife crises) and extreme traumas (e.g., grief, loss, depression, anxiety) involve a problem of narrative. For this reason, McAdams writes that "stories" literally "heal us when we are sick, and even move us toward psychological fulfillment and maturity."[8]

The importance of our stories also implies that they can become disruptive, pathological, self-defeating, or incoherent. One of my goals throughout these pages has been to suggest that a culture of scientism can engender various crises of narrative at both the individual and collective levels. This is particularly the case when the stories we tell repress their narrative elements and parade as fundamental empirical science. The story of society and human agency as a mechanics, susceptible to control and prediction by experts akin to those in the natural sciences, is a bad story. It is a bad story because it cannot accomplish what it promises (prediction). It is a bad story because it orients us toward manipulating the people around us as if they were objects (technocracy). And it is a bad story because it makes us particularly inarticulate and ill-equipped to deal with the world and the moral and political dimensions of our actions. So often the impact of those who speak in the name of "science" in the domain of human behavior is not illumination or better understanding of the world but distortion, blindness, and confusion. Scientism leads to bad decisions in economics, politics, foreign policy, and personal life. The foregoing chapters are in some senses a tour of the follies shaping our current moment.

Indeed, the high academic theory of social science makes a long, strange journey into ordinary, everyday culture and mass politics. On this journey it takes on a life of its own, such that what started out as science becomes something that is no longer under the control of its creators. The problem of ostensible sciences that take on a life of their own and create unforeseen consequences and problems is one of the central maladies of modern life.

In this respect, one of the key founding stories for the modern world is Mary Shelley's *Frankenstein*, the account of a young scientist and his creation of an artificial monster. A brilliant prodigy, Victor Frankenstein is sent by his family to study at a German university, where he develops a monomania for the new natural sciences of chemistry, physics, and particularly the problem of the origin and sources of life. Neglecting all other aspects of his life, Frankenstein's sole obsession becomes to discover what he calls the "hidden laws of nature" and the "physical secrets of the world."[9] Over the course of several years of feverish study and experimentation, he becomes the first person to uncover a science of the source of life, which allows him to artificially bestow "animation upon lifeless matter."[10] Sewing together parts of humans and other animals that he finds in dissection labs and slaughterhouses, the young scientist builds a hulking humanoid. But the scientific achievement that Frankenstein believed would endow him with everlasting fame and omniscience instead becomes a secret source of shame and terror when the monster escapes his control and embarks on a course of murder, destruction, and sorrow.

Victor Frankenstein's central delusion (like that of so many of us today) was that science would give people total control over reality. Shelley's genius was to see that the inventions and discoveries of science are never fully under the control of the scientist. Instead, the theories of science can take shape in monstrous form. The story of social science in the modern world—as with all sciences—is partly also a story of powers unleashed and dimly understood. Every one of the chapters in this book may be read as a certain weird retelling of the story of Frankenstein and his monster. Each is about science escaping the hands of its creators into something unintended, unexpected, unreasonable, and monstrous. This is especially true insofar as the theories of science lack humanistic dimensions—moral meanings, significance, and comprehension—and favor a cold, supposedly objective analysis. Indeed, Shelley depicts Frankenstein's monster as driven toward greater destruction precisely by the refusal of his creator to grapple with the human side of his creation. The monster continually begs to stop being mistreated and to be viewed in a fuller, more human light. Social scientists today (and we readers of social science) must also learn Frankenstein's lesson. We must learn to treat the creations of social science—its methodologies and theories—more humanistically. Failure to do so will mean that we will continue to inadvertently unleash monsters on the world.

Yet Shelley's mysterious tale was never a simple rejection of scientific advances. Shelley also saw that once created, the monster required compassion. Indeed, Frankenstein's monster asks that his tale—of how he escaped the bounds and intentions of his scientific creator—be heard. In the future, social scientific theories must also be weighed and carefully considered for what they contain of truth and authentic human ingenuity. Their tales must be heard. As the monster warns Frankenstein: "On you it rests, whether I quit forever the neighborhood of man and lead a harmless life, or become the scourge of your fellow creatures, and the author of your own speedy ruin."[11]

The brilliant myth of Frankenstein and his monster is also a story of science giving birth to something that it is often popularly thought to have banished: superstition, evil, darkness, ignorance, cruelty, and inhumanity. Even becoming conscious of the sources of error is often exceedingly difficult. This is because the fear of scientism and the abuse of scientific authority can sometimes lead to an even stronger attachment to the notion that scientific authority is a kind of omniscient savior. In the rush to overcome scientism and pseudoscience, we often run back to an unwitting embrace of the deeper sources of error (namely, an overestimation of the power of scientific reason). And in every attempt to free ourselves from pseudoscience, we might strengthen our ties to the underlying and mistaken assumptions.

Indeed, a culture of scientism helps produce a culture that also rejects genuine scientific authority. The scientism studied in these pages, by falsely trading on an authority it does not wield, helps to sow a wider skepticism and cynicism about the "elite" voices of scientists as such. A disturbing increase in science denial (e.g., conspiracy theorists, anti-vaxxers, climate change deniers) is in a mutually supporting dialectic with the absolute scientism of a Pinker or a Dawkins. Although they have not yet realized it, figures like Pinker and Dawkins, far from defending science, undermine it by overpromising and exaggerating its authority. Ultra-Darwinists and biblical literalists are dance partners.

The only way out of this dilemma that does not involve the dual irrationalisms of rejecting science and inflating the authority of science beyond reasonable bounds involves recovering other ways of knowing the world. One of the chief resources in this regard is the humanities. The humanities insist that there is an art to interpreting human behavior that is never reducible to a strict or exact science. Although it is not scientific, this art is not subjective or arbitrary, either.[12] Rather, it is an art practiced by many historians, literary scholars, cultural theorists, and even some rogue social scientists. Only the art of interpretation can begin to restore our culture to a clearer form of self-understanding that escapes the current delusions and disappointments of our reigning scientism. Only this will help correct the frightening tendency in our present hour to reject the rightful authority of natural science (e.g., ecology, vaccines) while at the same time submitting uncritically to the scientism of popular social theories (e.g., broken windows, *Homo economicus*). In the past of the humanities and interpretive disciplines lies a new future. But a key question remains: Where are the new humanists?

NOTES

INTRODUCTION: ELECTION DAY 2016

1. Michael Wolff, "Donald Trump Didn't Want to Be President; One Year Ago: The Plan to Lose, and the Administration's Shocked First Days," *New York*, January 3, 2018, http://nymag.com/intelligencer/2018/01/michael-wolff-fire-and-fury-book-donald-trump.html?gtm=bottom.

2. Nate Silver, "The Polls Are All Right," *FiveThirtyEight*, May 30, 2018, https://fivethirtyeight.com/features/the-polls-are-all-right/.

3. A. J. Ayer, *Language, Truth, and Logic*, 2nd ed. (New York: Dover Publications, 1952), 151, 48.

4. For a detailed philosophical defense of this view, see Mark Bevir and Jason Blakely, *Interpretive Social Science* (Oxford: Oxford University Press, 2018).

5. See Bruce Baum, *The Rise and Fall of the Caucasian Race: A Political History of Racial Identity* (New York: New York University Press, 2006), 50–94.

CHAPTER 1

1. Chris Mayer and Todd Sinai, "Bubble Trouble? Not Likely," *Wall Street Journal*, September 19, 2005, https://www.wsj.com/articles/SB112708454245544394.

2. Margaret Hwang Smith and Gary Smith, "Bubble, Bubble, Where's the Housing Bubble?," *Brookings Papers on Economic Activity* 1 (2006): 1–67.

3. Daniel Hirschman and Elizabeth Popp Berman, "Do Economists Make Policies? On the Political Effects of Economics," *Socio-Economic Review* 12 (2014): 781.

4. Richard Nadeau and Michael S. Lewis-Beck, "National Economic Voting in U.S. Presidential Elections," *Journal of Politics* 63, no. 1 (2001): 159–181.

5. Ray C. Fair, *Predicting Presidential Elections and Other Things* (Stanford, CA: Stanford University Press, 2002), 6.

6. For a path-breaking study of these rhetorical features (to which I am indebted), see Deirdre N. McCloskey, *The Rhetoric of Economics* (Madison: University of Wisconsin Press, 1998).

7. Mary S. Morgan, "Economics," in *The Cambridge History of Science: The Modern Social Sciences*, ed. Theodore Porter and Dorothy Ross (Cambridge, UK: Cambridge University Press 2003), 7:277.

8. See: Peter Wagner, "The Uses of the Social Sciences," in *The Cambridge History of Science*, 7:544–546.

9. Jennifer Jacobson, "Envying the Salaries of Economics Professors," *Chronicle of Higher Education*, June 6, 2002, https://www.chronicle. com/article/Envying-the-Salaries-of/46126.

10. Milton Friedman, "The Methodology of Positive Economics," in *The Philosophy of Economics*, 3rd ed., ed. Daniel Hausman (Cambridge, UK: Cambridge University Press, 2008), 153.

11. Philip Tetlock, *Expert Political Judgment: How Good Is It? How Can We Know?* (Princeton, NJ: Princeton University Press, 2005), 59, 247.

12. Tetlock, *Expert Political Judgment*, 54.

13. Tetlock, *Expert Political Judgment*, 54.

14. Adam Smith, *The Wealth of Nations*, ed. Edwin Cannan (Chicago: University of Chicago Press, 1976), 475, 477.

15. Friedrich Hayek, "The Use of Knowledge in Society," *American Economic Review* 35, no. 4 (1945): 527.

16. David Colander, Hans Föllmer, Armin Haas, Michael D. Goldberg, Katrina Juselius, Alan Kirman, Thomas Lux, and Birgitte Sloth, "The Financial Crisis and the Systematic Failure of Academic Economics," University of Copenhagen Department of Economics Discussion Paper No. 09-03 (March 9, 2009), https://papers.ssrn.com/sol3/papers. cfm?abstract_id=1355882.

17. Milton Friedman, "The Role of Government in Education," in *Capitalism and Freedom* (Chicago: University of Chicago Press, 2002), 91.

18. Friedman, "The Role of Government in Education," 91, 92–93.

19. Valerie Strauss, "To Trump's Education Pick, the U.S. Public School System is a 'Dead End,'" *Washington Post*, December 21, 2016, https://www.washingtonpost.com/news/answer-sheet/wp/2016/12/21/to-trumps-education-pick-the-u-s-public-school-system-is-a-dead-end/?utm_term=.e1e638830429.

20. See: Erin Einhorn, "The Extreme Sacrifice Detroit Parents Make to Access Better Schools," *Atlantic*, April 11, 2016, https://www.theatlantic.com/education/archive/2016/04/the-extreme-sacrifice-detroit-parents-make-to-access-better-schools/477585/; and Allie Gross, "Out of Options: School Choice Gutted Detroit's Public Schools," *Vice News*, December 18, 2016, https://news.vice.com/en_us/article/a3j5va/school-choice-detroit-betsy-devos.

21. Ian Whitaker, "A Case Study for Betsy DeVos's Education Utopia: Nevada's Failed Universal Voucher Program," *Atlantic*, February 2, 2017, https://www.theatlantic.com/education/archive/2017/02/can-a-universal-voucher-program-succeed/515436/.

22. Friedman, "The Role of Government in Education," 92.

CHAPTER 2

1. John Locke, *Second Treatise of Government*, ed. C. B. Macpherson (Indianapolis: Hackett Publishing, 1980), 28.

2. Locke, *Second Treatise of Government*, 28.

3. Adam Smith, *The Theory of Moral Sentiments* (Boston: Wells and Lilly, 1817), 120.

4. For the importance of rational choice, see Daniel Hausman, "Philosophy of Economics," in *Routledge Encyclopedia of Philosophy*, ed. Edward Craig (London: Routledge, 1998), 3:211–222.

5. Itzhak Gilboa, *Rational Choice* (Cambridge, MA: MIT Press, 2010), 39–40.

6. Gary S. Becker, *The Economic Approach to Human Behavior* (Chicago: University of Chicago Press, 1976), 14.

7. Steven D. Levitt and Stephen J. Dubner, "Bottom-Line Philanthropy," *New York Times*, March 9, 2008, https://www.nytimes.com/2008/03/09/magazine/09WWLN-freakonomics-t.html?_r=1&ref=magazine&oref=slogin.

8. Steven D. Levitt and Stephen J. Dubner, *Freakonomics* (New York: Harper Perennial, 2005), 73.

9.   Philip Cushman, "Why the Self Is Empty: Toward a Historically Situated Psychology," *American Psychologist* 45, no. 5 (1990): 599–611.

10. Jonathan Van Meter, "Ivanka Trump Knows What It Means to Be a Modern Millennial," *Vogue*, February 24, 2015, https://www.vogue.com/article/ivanka-trump-collection-the-apprentice-family.

11. Robert Bellah, *Habits of the Heart: Individualism and Commitment in American Life* (Berkeley: University of California Press, 2007), 91.

12. In the following analysis of Mayhew I have drawn from research conducted with Chase Mendoza.

13. David R. Mayhew, *Congress: The Electoral Connection* (New Haven, CT: Yale University Press, 2004), 5.

14. David R. Mayhew, "Observations on 'Congress: The Electoral Connection' a Quarter Century after Writing It," *Political Science and Politics* 34, no. 2 (2001): 251.

15. James Buchanan, "Why Does Government Grow?," in *Budgets and Bureaucrats*, ed. Thomas Borcherding (Durham, NC: Duke University Press, 1977), 3–18.

16. James Buchanan and Gordon Tullock, *The Calculus of Consent* (Ann Arbor: University of Michigan Press, 1965), 295; see also: xvii, 28–29, 294–296.

17. Bruce Bueno de Mesquita and Alastair Smith, *The Dictator's Handbook: Why Bad Behavior Is Almost Always Good Politics* (New York: PublicAffairs, 2011), 10, xxiv.

18. Bueno de Mesquita and Smith, *The Dictator's Handbook*, 8.

19. Bueno de Mesquita and Smith, *The Dictator's Handbook*, x, xxv.

20. See: John Rawls, *A Theory of Justice* (Cambridge, MA: Harvard University Press, 1971).

21. Gordon Wood offers a vivid example of this older republican ethos in revolutionary America. Wood notes that the concept of the "customer" did not exist at this time; instead the notion of the "patron" was dominant. Patrons had highly personal, ongoing relationships of social trust with those with whom they conducted commerce. Instead of maximizing economic advantage on an impersonal market, the patron often favored familiar relationships with other business owners and traders with "little or no awareness at any one moment of profitability." Gordon Wood, *The Radicalism of the American Revolution* (New York: Vintage Books, 1993), 67.

22. James Buchanan, *Public Choice: The Origins and Development of a Research Program* (Fairfax, VA: Center for Study of Public Choice, 2003), 11.

23. The most famous of these criticisms have been articulated by behavioral psychologists mentioned previously. For an early list of violations of rational axioms, see Amos Tversky and Daniel Kahneman, "Advances in Prospect Theory: Cumulative Representation of Uncertainty," *Journal of Risk and Uncertainty* 5 (1992): 298.

24. Milton Friedman, "The Methodology of Positive Economics," in *The Philosophy of Economics*, 3rd ed., ed. Daniel Hausman (Cambridge, UK: Cambridge University Press, 2008), 146.

CHAPTER 3

1. Thomas Hobbes, *Leviathan*, ed. Richard Tuck (Cambridge, UK: Cambridge University Press, 1996), 9.

2. Julien Offray de La Mettrie, *Man a Machine* (La Salle, IL: Open Court, 1912), 141, 93, 132.

3. B. F. Skinner, "B. F. Skinner Says What's Wrong with the Social Sciences," *Listener*, September 30, 1971, 431.

4. Paul Churchland, "Eliminative Materialism and the Propositional Attitudes," *Journal of Philosophy* 78, no. 2 (1981): 90.

5. Steven Pinker, *How the Mind Works* (New York: W. W. Norton, 1997), 76.

6. Pinker, *How the Mind Works*, 76.

7. Pinker, *How the Mind Works*, 26, 27.

8. Steven Pinker, *The Blank Slate: The Modern Denial of Human Nature* (New York: Penguin, 2002), 41.

9. Steven Pinker, "How to Think About the Mind," *Newsweek*, September 27, 2004, 78.

10. Alec Coppen, "The Biochemistry of Affective Disorders," *British Journal of Psychiatry* 113 (1967): 1237.

11. Erin Shumaker, "How Vintage Advertisements Got Depression Totally Wrong," *HuffPost*, December 7, 2017, https://www.huffpost.com/entry/antidepressants-advertisements-women_n_7276906.

12. Nathan Greenslit and Ted Kaptchuk, "Antidepressants and Advertising: Psychopharmaceuticals in Crisis," *Yale Journal of Biology and Medicine* 85 (2012): 157.

13. See: Irving Kirsch, *The Emperor's New Drugs: Exploding the Antidepressant Myth* (New York: Basic Books, 2010), 3.

14. Peter D. Kramer, *Listening to Prozac: A Psychiatrist Explores Antidepressant Drugs and the Remaking of the Self* (New York: Viking, 1993), xix.

15. Kramer, *Listening to Prozac*, 300.

16. Gary Greenberg, *Manufacturing Depression: The Secret History of a Modern Disease* (New York: Simon & Schuster, 2010).

17. Oliver James, *The Selfish Capitalist: Origins of Affluenza* (London: Vermilion, 2008).

18. Gregg Henriques, "ADHD and the Problem of the Double Hermeneutic," *Psychology Today*, December 17, 2013, https://www.psychologytoday.com/us/blog/theory-knowledge/201312/adhd-and-the-problem-the-double-hermeneutic.

19. John Alford, Carolyn Funk, and John Hibbing, "Are Political Orientations Genetically Transmitted?," *American Political Science Review* 99, no. 2 (2005): 163.

20. Alford, Funk, and Hibbing, "Are Political Orientations Genetically Transmitted?," 164.

21. John Searle, "Minds, Brains, and Programs," *Behavioral and Brain Sciences* 3, no. 3 (1980): 417–424.

22. Charles Taylor, "Cognitive Psychology," in *Human Agency and Language*, Philosophical Papers 1 (Cambridge, UK: Cambridge University Press, 1985), 197, 193–194.

23. Joseph Stalin, *Dialectical and Historical Materialism* (New York, NY: International Publishers, 1940), 15, 30.

CHAPTER 4

1. See Hanne Andersen and Brian Hepburn, "Scientific Method," in *The Stanford Encyclopedia of Philosophy*, summer 2016 ed., ed. Edward N. Zalta, https://plato.stanford.edu/archives/sum2016/entries/scientific-method/.

2. Brian Christian and Tom Griffiths, *Algorithms to Live By: The Computer Science of Human Decisions* (New York: Henry Holt, 2016), 14.

3. Christian and Griffiths, *Algorithms to Live By*, 15.

4. Olivia Fox Cabane, *The Charisma Myth: How Anyone Can Master the Art and Science of Personal Magnetism* (New York: Penguin, 2012), 6–7.

5. Richard Thaler and Cass Sunstein, *Nudge: Improving Decisions About Health, Wealth, and Happiness* (New Haven, CT: Yale University Press, 2008), 19.

6. Thaler and Sunstein, *Nudge*, 6.

7. Thaler and Sunstein, *Nudge*, 37.

8. Thaler and Sunstein, *Nudge*, 20, 37.

9. Steven Pinker, *How the Mind Works* (New York: W. W. Norton, 1997), 69, 365, 64, 25, 59.

CHAPTER 5

1. See David Horn, *The Criminal Body: Lombroso and the Anatomy of Deviance* (New York: Routledge, 2003), 1.

2. Khalil Gibran Muhammad, *The Condemnation of Blackness* (Cambridge, MA: Harvard University Press, 2010).

3. For an excellent detailed account of this shift, see Elizabeth Hinton, *From the War on Poverty to the War on Crime* (Cambridge, MA: Harvard University Press, 2016).

4. Charles Murray, Foreword to *Thinking About Crime*, ed. James Q. Wilson (New York: Basic Books, 2013), xvii.

5. James Q. Wilson and Richard Herrnstein, *Crime and Human Nature* (New York: The Free Press, 1985), 56.

6. James Q. Wilson and George Kelling, "Broken Windows: The Police and Neighborhood Safety," in *Thinking About Crime*, 65.

7. Wilson and Kelling, "Broken Windows," 67.

8.   Bernard Harcourt, "Policing Disorder," *Boston Review* (2002), http:// bostonreview.net/archives/BR27.2/harcourt.html.

9. Michelle Alexander, *The New Jim Crow* (New York: The New Press, 2010), 7; see also 5–8, 40–57.

10. Wilson and Herrnstein, *Crime and Human Nature*, 148, 167.

11. Wilson and Herrnstein, *Crime and Human Nature*, 374.

12. Peter Kraska, "Crime Control as Warfare," in *Militarizing the American Criminal Justice System*, ed. Peter Kraska (Boston: Northeastern University Press, 2001), 23.

13. Jamiles Lartey, "By the Numbers: U.S. Police Kill More in Days Than Other Countries Do in Years," *Guardian*, June 9, 2015, https:// www.theguardian.com/us-news/2015/jun/09/the-counted-police- killings-us-vs-other-countries.

14. Sam Levin, "Hundreds Dead, No One Charged: The Uphill Battle against Los Angeles Police Killings," *Guardian*, August 24, 2018, https://www.theguardian.com/us-news/2018/aug/24/los-angeles -police-violence-shootings-african-american.

15. Peter Kraska, "Playing War," in *Militarizing the American Criminal Justice System*, 144–145.

16. Wilson and Herrnstein, *Crime and Human Nature*, 469.

17. Wilson and Herrnstein, *Crime and Human Nature*, 485.
18. Aaron Panofsky, *Misbehaving Science* (Chicago: University of Chicago Press, 2014), 193.
19. Stuart Hall, *Race, the Floating Signifier* (Northampton, MA: Media Education Foundation, 1997), https://www.mediaed.org/transcripts/Stuart-Hall-Race-the-Floating-Signifier-Transcript.pdf.
20. Hall, *Race, the Floating Signifier*.
21. Sean Sullivan, "Donald Trump Says 'Profiling' Might Be Needed to Fight Terrorism," *Chicago Tribune*, September 19, 2016, https://www.chicagotribune.com/nation-world/ct-donald-trump-profiling-20160919-story.html.
22. See: Bernard Harcourt, *Illusion of Order: The False Promise of Broken Windows Policing* (Cambridge, MA: Harvard University Press, 2001).

CHAPTER 6

1. George W. Bush, "Remarks to United States and Coalition Troops at Bagram Air Base, Afghanistan, March 1, 2006," in *Public Papers of the Presidents of the United States: George W. Bush* (Washington, DC: United States Government Printing Office, 2010), 375.
2. Daniel Immerwahr, *How to Hide an Empire: A History of the Greater United States* (New York: Farrar, Straus, and Giroux, 2019).
3. Francis Fukuyama, *The End of History and the Last Man* (New York: Simon & Schuster, 2006), xi–xii.
4. Fukuyama, *The End of History and the Last Man*, 48.
5. Fukuyama, *The End of History and the Last Man*, 73, 72.
6. William Kristol et al., "Letter to President Bush on the War on Terrorism," *Project for the New American Century*, September 20, 2001, http://www.newamericancentury.org/Bushletter.htm.
7. Michael W. Doyle, "Kant, Liberal Legacies, and Foreign Affairs," in *Debating the Democratic Peace*, ed. Michael Brown, Sean Lynn-Jones, and Steven Miller (Cambridge, MA: The MIT Press, 2001), 10.
8. Doyle, "Kant, Liberal Legacies, and Foreign Affairs," 54.
9. Doyle, "Kant, Liberal Legacies, and Foreign Affairs," 31.
10. Immerwahr, *How to Hide an Empire*, 385.
11. For a discussion of the repressed ethical questions about this new form of warfare, see John R. Emery, "Killer Robots: Algorithmic Warfare and Techno-Ethics," *Platypus: Committee on the Anthropology of Science, Technology and Computing*, March 7, 2018, https://www.blog.castac.org/2018/03/killer-robots
12. This was particularly true of versions of the theory that had more permissive definitions of democracy. See Sean Lynn-Jones, Preface to *Debating the Democratic Peace*, xvii.

13. Samuel Huntington, "The Clash of Civilizations?," *Foreign Affairs* 72, no. 3 (1993): 26, 24.

14. Huntington, "The Clash of Civilizations?," 25.

15. Huntington, "The Clash of Civilizations?," 31, 35.

16. Huntington, "The Clash of Civilizations?," 24, 22, 25.

17. Huntington, "The Clash of Civilizations?", 35, 38.

18. Richard Dawkins, *The Selfish Gene* (Oxford: Oxford University Press, 2006).

19. Richard Dawkins, *The God Delusion* (New York: Houghton Mifflin Harcourt, 2006), 219.

20. Dawkins, *The God Delusion*, 303, 298.

21. Dawkins, *The God Delusion*, 307.

22. Dawkins, *The God Delusion*, 315, 316.

CONCLUSION

1. Czeslaw Milosz, "Inside and Outside," in *Road-Side Dog* (New York: Farrar, Straus and Giroux, 1998), 200–201.

2. For a wider discussion, to which I am indebted, see Deirdre N. McCloskey, *The Rhetoric of Economics* (Madison: University of Wisconsin Press, 1985).

3. Louis James, "The Beginnings of a New Type of Popular Fiction: Plagiarisms of Dickens," in *Dickens and Victorian Print Cultures*, ed. Robert L. Patten (New York: Routledge, 2016), 189.

4. Martin Heidegger, *The Question Concerning Technology*, trans. William Lovitt (New York: Garland Publishing, 1977), 17.

5. Heidegger, *The Question Concerning Technology*, 14.

6. Heidegger, *The Question Concerning Technology*, 21.

7. Hans-Georg Gadamer, "Hermeneutics and Social Science," *Cultural Hermeneutics* 2, no. 4 (1975): 316.

8. Dan McAdams, *The Stories We Live By* (New York: Guildford Press, 1993), 31. See also Dan McAdams, "The Psychology of Life Stories," *Review of General Psychology* 5, no. 2 (2001): 100–122.

9. Mary Shelley, *Frankenstein* (Mineola, NY: Dover Publications, 1994), 18, 19.

10. Shelley, *Frankenstein*, 31.

11. Shelley, *Frankenstein*, 70.

12. For a fuller defense of this view, see Mark Bevir and Jason Blakely, *Interpretive Social Science* (Oxford: Oxford University Press, 2018), 54–60.

For the benefit of digital users, indexed terms that span two pages (e.g., 52–53) may, on occasion, appear on only one of those pages.

CPSIA information can be obtained
at www.ICGtesting.com
Printed in the USA
BVHW032128130222
628544BV00006B/3